MONA SUTTON

100 Engaging Short Stories for Senior Women

Contents

INTRODUCTION

Welcome to *"100 Engaging Short Stories for Senior Women"*!

This book has been created especially for you, for those who have entered the mature season of life and wish to rediscover the excitement of reliving past experiences, smiling in the present, and reflecting on what has been and what is yet to come.

The pages in front of you contain a treasure of carefully selected stories designed to stimulate your mind, offer moments of enjoyment, and give you a feeling of inner well-being. We know how important it is to spend quality time, and with these 100 stories, we hope to take you on an exciting journey filled with laughter, smiles, and deep reflection.

Each story is a bridge to the past, an invitation to dive into the depths of memories. You can relive extraordinary adventures, meet unforgettable characters and immerse yourself in faraway places, all without leaving the comfort of your favorite armchair. Experience the thrill of past emotions, rediscover the nuances of your most treasured experiences, and dive into a world of wonder through these pages.

But this book doesn't just stop at the past. It will make you smile and laugh like you used to, brightening your day with cheerfulness and lightness. The humorous stories will bring a smile to your face, the comic moments will make you burst laughing.

ENJOY YOUR BONUS!

CHAPTER 1 A Wonderful Gift

Once upon a time in the vibrant city of Manhattan, the clock struck 7 a.m., and Serena's day was about to take an exhilarating turn! Her heart danced with expectation, excitement, and just a tiny bit of nervousness as she watched the sun begin its ascent over the world. You see, this was no ordinary day for Serena; she had been eagerly anticipating this moment for a whole nine months – the birth of her first child, little Alicia. Serena was a dynamic blend of cultures, hailing from both Spain and America, and she had found her perfect match in Paul, a charming Spaniard. As she made her way to the hospital, she wasn't alone in this adventure. Her spirited mother, supportive sister, and the ever-calm Paul were all right there with her, forming a cheer squad of love and laughter in the delivery room.

In the midst of contractions and anticipation, the room resonated with joy and humor. Serena's mother, a natural storyteller, was spinning hilarious tales that made everyone laugh, while Paul, holding Serena's hand, offered the unwavering comfort and relaxation she needed. With each surge of determination, Serena pushed with all her might. Time seemed to stretch and twist, and what felt like just a couple of minutes turned into an epic journey in the eyes of her loved ones present. The labor pains were no joke, but Serena was a fierce warrior, reminding herself of the incredible joy awaiting her at the finish line. Pushing harder than she ever thought possible, she embraced the powerful surge of motherly strength that surged through her.

And then, at precisely 7:36 a.m., little Alicia officially entered the world, like a burst of sunlight illuminating their lives. Tears of joy streamed down Serena and Paul's faces; they couldn't believe they were now parents! Despite being grown-ups, they still felt like kids, embarking on an unforgettable adventure of parenthood. Alicia's tiny face was an absolute bundle of cuteness and vitality, and as she let out her first cries, Serena held her daughter in awe, tears of happiness mixing with her own. It was a moment she had dreamed of, cherished in her heart for so long. Through teary eyes, she turned to her mom and said, "I am so happy; I love her with all my heart and more!" Her emotions overflowed like a bubbling fountain of love and joy.

Her mom and grandma had told her about the magical power of motherhood and the unbreakable bond between parent and child, but it was only in this moment, cradling her precious bundle, that Serena truly understood the depth of that connection. Years flew by like leaves in the wind, and little Alicia grew into a strong and loving woman, embarking on her own journey of motherhood. Serena's heart swelled with pride and joy as she witnessed her daughter embrace this new chapter of life. With Alicia now a mother herself, Serena found herself becoming a grandmother. Her heart burst with happiness as she held her grandson in her arms, relishing the cycle of life continuing before her eyes. The stories of her own mother and grandmother now found their place in the pages of Serena's life, and she embraced the role of a loving mentor, sharing wisdom and tales of motherhood with her daughter, just as it had been done for generations.

Surrounded by her family's laughter, love, and promise of a brighter tomorrow, Serena felt gratitude filling every fiber of her being. Each moment spent with her loved ones was a cherished treasure, and she knew that the love they had woven together would endure for generations to come. As the sun set on another beautiful day, Serena looked out at the city lights of Manhattan, marveling at the remarkable journey life had taken her on. She knew that every moment, every laugh, every tear, and every hug was a precious gift from the universe. In the loving embrace of her family, she found comfort and strength, knowing that the legacy of love they were building would stretch far beyond their lifetimes. And with the promise of a brand new day on the horizon, she thanked the universe for the beautiful gift of love that had woven their lives together, forever and always.

As the story of Serena and her family continues to unfold, one thing is certain – love will forever be the heartwarming melody that carries them through each chapter, dancing through life with laughter and joy. And so, they live happily ever after, for love knows no boundaries, and its light shines brighter with each generation.

CHAPTER 2 Ginger and Riley

Ginger is a very happy and friendly dog. He once witnessed a baby bird fall from its nest while he was strolling in the park. Max sprinted over to it and carefully placed it in his mouth. He brought it to safety under a tree, where he then stood watch over it. Ginger asked the bird, "What is your name?" and the bird replied "Riley" in a very shy way, probably intimidated by the dog. Riley was very grateful for being saved by Ginger and thanked him.

With each passing day, Ginger and Riley's bond grew stronger. They spent countless hours together, exploring the park and its wonders. Riley would perch on Ginger's back as they roamed the green fields, their friendship becoming the talk of the park regulars.

One sunny afternoon, they encountered a group of children playing catch. Ginger and Riley decided to join in the fun. Riley would fly around, and Ginger would try to catch the ball in his mouth. The kids were amazed by the incredible teamwork and coordination between the unlikely friends.

Their adventures weren't limited to the park alone. Ginger's owner, a kind-hearted woman named Emily, welcomed Riley into their home with open arms. She set up a cozy nest for the little bird and made sure he felt comfortable. Ginger and Riley spent evenings curled up together, listening to the soft hum of Emily's voice as she read them bedtime stories.

As time went on, their friendship became an inseparable part of their lives. Ginger would often escort Riley to different parts of the park, showing him the best spots to find worms and insects. In return, Riley would teach Ginger songs and melodies he had learned from his bird family. They became the ultimate duo, and everyone who crossed their path couldn't help but smile at the sight of a playful dog and a chirping bird, side by side. People would often bring treats for Ginger and seeds for Riley, acknowledging the joy they brought to the park community.

During one winter, a heavy snowfall covered the park, turning it into a winter wonderland. Ginger and Riley were ecstatic and wasted no time in building a snow fort together. They would take turns rolling in the snow and playfully chasing each other, leaving behind a trail of laughter and happiness.

As years passed, their friendship only deepened. Their story became legendary, with families from far and wide coming to the park to catch a glimpse of the famous duo. Ginger and Riley became symbols of hope, proving that true friendship knows no boundaries and can defy even the most unlikely circumstances.

Their journey together continued to inspire everyone they encountered. Local newspapers featured their heartwarming story, and soon, the entire city knew about the inseparable bond between a dog and a little bird.

In their golden years, Ginger and Riley still visited the park daily, though at a slower pace. Their eyes reflected a lifetime of memories shared, adventures undertaken, and love that had stood the test of time. And so, with wagging tails and melodious tunes, Ginger and Riley's legacy lived on, reminding the world that sometimes the most extraordinary friendships can emerge from the simplest of encounters. In a world full of differences, they taught us that love and compassion can unite even the most unlikely of hearts. As the years turned, their story remained etched in the hearts of those who had witnessed the incredible journey of two souls who found their best friend in the most unexpected of places.

CHAPTER 3 "What's for dinner?"

Sam was an old man, well into his golden years, and he spent his days following a predictable routine. From the moment the sun peeked through the curtains, painting the room with a warm glow, Sam would reach for the newspapers stacked neatly on the coffee table. He'd leisurely skim through the headlines, absorbing the happenings of the world, one article at a time.

With the morning news digested, Sam would often find himself drifting into the land of dreams, indulging in afternoon naps that offered a brief escape from the rigors of reality. These siestas became his private sanctuary, a time to rest his weary bones and to dream of adventures from the days of his youth.

But the highlight of Sam's day was the evening. As the soft light of dusk embraced their cozy home, his beloved wife, Josephine, would return from her day of activity and exuberance. Josephine was a ball of energy, a whirlwind of joy and enthusiasm. She loved engaging in various activities, but above all, she adored dancing. Her feet could effortlessly glide across the floor as if they were buoyed by the very rhythm of life itself. Josephine often complained about Sam's seemingly lazy lifestyle. She would affectionately tease him, saying, "You're like a sloth in a rocking chair, dear! All you do is read, sleep, and watch TV." Sam would just chuckle and pat her hand, appreciating her concern while cherishing the simplicity of his own pursuits.

However, as the years went by, Sam began to notice subtle changes in Josephine's hearing. He couldn't bear the thought of her missing out on the joys of conversation and the melodious tunes of the world around her. With a heavy heart, he decided to take action and talk to a doctor about it. Setting an appointment for Josephine was not easy, as the doctor's schedule was packed for the next month. But Sam remained patient and determined to address his wife's hearing concerns. Finally, the day of the appointment arrived, and they set off to see the specialist.

The doctor greeted them warmly, and after a thorough examination, the doctor recommended a simple test for Josephine's hearing. He suggested that Sam stand at a distance from Josephine, about 30-40 feet away, and gradually get closer while speaking in a normal tone of voice. If Josephine heard his words clearly, it would indicate that her hearing was still sharp.

That evening, as Josephine was bustling around the kitchen, preparing a delicious dinner, Sam seized the opportunity to conduct the doctor's test. He positioned himself in the living room, where he often read his newspapers, and called out to his wife, "Honey, what's for dinner?" No answer reached his ears, and Sam decided to try again, raising his voice a little louder this time. "Honey, what's for dinner?" he called, hoping to get a response. But once again, Josephine seemed oblivious to his question. Determined to get to the bottom of the situation, Sam inched closer, moving step by step towards the kitchen while repeating the same inquiry. Yet, no matter how near he got, Josephine appeared to be engrossed in her culinary creations, unaware of her husband's attempts to engage her in conversation.

Finally, when Sam was mere meters away from Josephine, he mustered up the last of his hope and asked again, "Honey, what's for dinner?" He held his breath, praying for a response. This time, to his surprise and slight amusement, Josephine turned around with a beaming smile and said, "Sam! For the 6th time, it's pasta!" Her eyes twinkled with mirth, and Sam couldn't help but chuckle at the situation. Relieved that Josephine could hear him after all, Sam wrapped his arms around her lovingly. "I'm sorry, my dear. I just wanted to be sure," he said, feeling a mix of affection and playfulness. Josephine leaned into his embrace, her laughter echoing through the air. "Oh, you worry too much, my old bear. I can hear just fine! Now, let's sit down and enjoy our pasta together."

And so, the couple settled down to savor their dinner, basking in the comfort of each other's presence. For in the symphony of their lives, they knew that while Sam's days may be quieter and filled with quieter joys, they were perfectly complemented by Josephine's exuberance and love for life's vibrant dance. Together, they created a harmony that ranscended age and time, proving that in love, there is always a way to bridge any gap - be it of distance or hearing.

CHAPTER 4 "Do you know who I am?"

A famous Hollywood actor decides to come back to his hometown for Christmas to spend time with his kids and grandchildren. Since he is spending some days in the city, he also decides to visit a nursing home where some of his childhood friends currently live. He heard from them a few years back, and some of his friends have dementia or Alzheimer's, and he wonders whether he will be recognized by them.

As soon as he steps into the building, his friends, and not only, greet him with a lot of enthusiasm. He is excited to see people he spent his childhood with as they talk about old stories of when they were teenagers. They spend many hours talking and laughing, having a good time reminiscing about the good old days.

Many other elderly men and women are also excited to meet him as they watch TV shows and movies of him, taking advantage of the opportunity to ask him questions about movies and his career. The actor feels humbled by their admiration and takes the time to engage with each person, sharing anecdotes from his life in Hollywood and listening intently to their own life stories.

However, there is one man who does not appear to be aware of him. This surprises the actor, but it doesn't deter him from making a connection. He decides to approach the man with genuine warmth and kindness.

He says, "Hey, how are you doing? Merry Christmas!"

To which the man replies with "Good, thank you. How are you? Merry Christmas to you too," seeming surprised by this stranger coming to talk to him.

The celebrity then asked, "Do you know who I am?"

And the gentleman goes, "No, but if you ask the nurse, she will tell you what your name is" with a smile.

The actor's heart is filled with compassion as he realizes that this man's memory might not be what it used to be. Instead of feeling hurt or disappointed, he sees an opportunity to create a new memory, to bring a moment of happiness to this fellow resident.

With a warm smile, the actor introduces himself, sharing stories of their shared past, describing the mischief they got into as kids, the games they played, and the dreams they once had. The man's eyes light up as he listens, and though he may not fully grasp who the actor is, he feels a connection to the shared experiences of their youth.

Throughout the day, the actor spends time with his old friends, engaging in activities, and enjoying the simple joys of the season. He discovers that the power of human connection transcends fame and memory, and that the love and joy they share with each other are what truly matter.

As he leaves the nursing home that evening, the actor is filled with a profound sense of gratitude. He cherishes the time he spent with his childhood friends, whether they remembered him or not. He realizes that this visit has been a gift not only to them but also to himself. He experienced the true meaning of Christmas – the spirit of giving, of love, and of making meaningful connections that touch the heart and soul. And so, as the actor returns to his family, he carries with him the warmth and memories of his time spent in that nursing home. He knows that no matter how famous or successful one may become, it is the genuine connections we make with others that leave a lasting impact on our lives. The magic of Christmas is not found in the glitz and glamour of Hollywood, but in the love and laughter shared with those we hold dear.

CHAPTER 5 Apples

An 8-year-old girl is waiting eagerly for her nanny to join her for breakfast. It has become their special morning ritual, and the little girl couldn't wait to share this moment with her beloved grandma. As soon as she wakes up, she rushes to the kitchen and settles into her usual chair, her eyes fixed on the bowl of colorful fruits in front of her.

Without hesitation, she grabs two apples and a handful of blueberries. The blueberries look so tempting, and she can't resist popping a few into her mouth as she waits for her nanny to prepare the pancakes.

The grandma, with her warm and loving smile, walks over to the little girl and says, "My love, could you please pass me one of those apples so I can sit next to you while we wait for breakfast to be ready?" She looks forward to cherishing this moment with her granddaughter, savoring the love they share.

However, instead of sharing one of the apples, the little girl starts biting into both apples, one after the other, almost in a hurry. The grandma's smile wavers as she notices her granddaughter's behavior. She had hoped for a moment of togetherness, but the girl seems engrossed in her own little world. After taking one bite from each apple, the young girl suddenly has a change of heart. She realizes the joy of sharing with her grandma and seeing her smile. With a bright twinkle in her eyes, she gives one of the apples to her nanny and says, "This is for you! This one tastes better and it's sweeter. I want you to have it."

The grandma's heart melts with happiness, and her smile returns, even brighter than before. She embraces her granddaughter with a warm hug, touched by the little girl's thoughtfulness and her willingness to share. In that simple act of giving, the young girl not only shared a sweet apple but also the sweetness of her heart.

From that day on, every morning, they continued their breakfast routine. The little girl enjoyed the pancakes her nanny lovingly made, and the grandma cherished every moment spent with her granddaughter. They talked about school, dreams, and shared stories of their adventures together.

As the years passed, the little girl grew older, but the bond between her and her nanny only grew stronger. They continued to create cherished memories together, embracing each day with love and gratitude for the simple joys that life brings.

And in the kitchen, amidst the aroma of pancakes and the bowl of fruits, a sweet tradition continued, symbolizing the enduring love between a granddaughter and her beloved nanny. For in the simplicity of their breakfast ritual, they found the beauty of connection, and their hearts remained forever intertwined in a love that knew no bounds.

Years later, when the little girl had grown into a strong and independent young woman, she still treasured those moments in the kitchen with her nanny. The memories of those shared breakfasts became a source of comfort and a reminder of the love that had shaped her life. As she stood in her own kitchen one morning, preparing pancakes for her own family, she couldn't help but smile at the memory of that special morning when she had given her nanny the sweeter apple. In that moment, she realized the profound impact of simple acts of love and kindness.

And so, the legacy of love continued, passed down through generations, as the little girl, now a grown woman, embraced her own family with the same warmth and affection she had experienced from her beloved grandma. The bond they had shared remained etched in her heart, reminding her that love, in all its sweetness, is the true treasure of life.

CHAPTER 6 The American Businessman and the Mexican fisherman.

An American businessman goes to a small village in Mexico for a holiday with his wife. As the couple walks by the beach, the businessman notices a little stand where a Mexican man is selling fish to people, and he says, "Good morning! Wow, those fishes look fresh and delicious! How long does it take you to fish them?"

The fisherman says, "It depends on the day…but not much."

Intrigued, the businessman continues the conversation, "Why don't you spend more time fishing? You would get more fish."

The Mexican man looks out at the vast expanse of the ocean and smiles warmly, "You see, señor, the quantity of fish I catch every day is enough to satisfy not only my own needs but also those of my family. I have all that I need, and it is not necessary to do more than that."

Curiosity piqued, the American businessman inquires further, "How do you spend the rest of your time, then?"

With a big smile that radiates contentment, the Mexican man replies, "Well, señor, I lead a simple and fulfilling life. After I wake up in the morning, I head out to the sea with my boat and fish for a bit. It's a peaceful time to connect with nature and my surroundings. Then, I return home and spend quality time playing with my kids, watching them grow and learn. In the afternoon, I take a siesta with my wife, a moment of rest and togetherness. Later on, I stroll down to the village, where I share good times with my friends. We enjoy a drink or two, and I even play my guitar, filling the air with music and laughter. At the end of the day, I come back home to spend precious moments with my family. I try to fully appreciate life's simple joys and cherish the love and happiness around me."

The tourist is captivated by the Mexican man's contentment and simplicity. However, he can't help but share his thoughts, "Look, I do not mean to teach you how to conduct your life, but I can't help but see great potential in your fishing business. You could achieve so much more. First, I believe you would benefit from staying in the sea and working longer hours. Waking up earlier would help you catch more fish and increase your profit. Eventually, you could sell your boat and buy a bigger one so that you have more space for the fish you sell. As you catch lots of fish every day, you will be able to sell to big shops and not just to individual customers, leading to even higher income. With your dedication and hard work, you could even open your own fish business. The possibilities are endless, and you could make a lot of money. Imagine yourself as the CEO of a thriving business in a big city like Los Angeles or New York..."

The fisherman seems excited by the idea and asks, "I understand, and it sounds like a great plan... but how long would it take me to achieve all these goals?"

The businessman's eyes gleam with enthusiasm, "Ah, you see, it's a project with enormous potential, and its results will blow your mind! It might take you around ten to fifteen years of hard work and dedication, but in the end, the financial rewards will be immense!"

The Mexican listens carefully, considering the businessman's proposition. "Ok, what then?" he asks.

With an even bigger smile, the businessman replies, "That is exactly the point where all your effort will pay off. You will have made millions... or even billions!"

As the Mexican imagines the life of financial abundance, his mind drifts into a realm of possibilities. He envisions himself living in luxury, surrounded by everything money can buy. The American businessman continues, "And then when you have all that money, you will be able to retire and live life on your terms. You can come back to a small village, like this one, and enjoy the beach life once again. Sleeping late, playing with your kids, taking siestas, spending time with friends, and fully appreciating life's simple pleasures."

The Mexican's gaze shifts from the illusion of a grand future back to his current reality. He reflects on the peace and joy he already finds in his simple life, surrounded by loved ones, the soothing sound of the waves, and the fresh sea breeze. With newfound clarity, he looks at the businessman and says, "Señor, I thank you for your advice, but I am content with my life just as it is. I have all that I need, and I am surrounded by the people I love. Money and material possessions do not hold the same value for me as the richness of the simple moments that bring happiness to my heart. I have already found wealth in the love and joy that fills my everyday life. There is no need for me to chase after more."

The businessman is taken aback by the Mexican man's wisdom and contentment. He realizes that sometimes, in the pursuit of more, we may overlook the riches we already possess. As the sun sets over the horizon, painting the sky with a canvas of colors, the American businessman walks back to his luxurious hotel, his mind filled with reflections on the encounter with the fisherman. And while the possibilities of wealth and success are still enticing, a seed of appreciation for life's simple joys begins to take root in his heart, reminding him that true abundance can be found in the moments of love, connection, and contentment that grace each day.

CHAPTER 7 "What are you doing?"

Angelo, the young and adventurous truck driver, found himself at a quirky truck stop in a remote petrol station, ready to answer nature's call. Little did he know that this mundane bathroom break would soon turn into a comical tale that he would cherish forever. As he approached the restrooms, Angelo noticed the "Occupied" sign hanging on the first one. Not wanting to wait, he strolled confidently into the second bathroom, hoping for a little privacy.

But as soon as he settled onto the toilet seat, he heard a mysterious voice coming from the other bathroom stall. "Hello, how are you?" the voice cheerfully inquired. Now, normally, Angelo wasn't the type to strike up conversations with strangers, especially not while handling business in the restroom. But that day, he was feeling exceptionally buoyant and decided to play along. "I'm doing great! How about you?" he replied with a grin. To his surprise, the voice from the other stall continued the banter, asking, "And what are you doing in there?" Angelo couldn't believe his ears. This was getting downright bizarre! But hey, he was in a good mood, so why not have some fun? He chuckled and answered, "Well, my friend, I guess I'm doing the same thing you are – taking a poop!"

Suddenly, the tone in the other stall changed, and a wave of irritation swept over the stranger. Angelo could hear some colorful language being muttered, and then the guy snapped, "Look, I'll call you back later. There's a fool next door who's answering all my questions!" Angelo burst into laughter, unable to contain the hilarity of the situation. Who would have thought that he'd become an unwitting participant in a restroom phone call exchange? As he finished up and washed his hands, he couldn't stop chuckling at the absurdity of being dubbed the "question-answering fool" by someone he'd never met.

From that day forward, whenever Angelo pulled into a truck stop, he couldn't help but smile as he recalled that unforgettable encounter. It became his go-to funny story, one he eagerly shared with friends and fellow truck drivers during their long journeys on the road. Every time he recounted the tale, laughter filled the air, and it felt like that random bathroom encounter had turned into a legendary road trip legend. Life has an uncanny way of surprising us with moments of lightheartedness and amusement, even in the most ordinary places. For Angelo, that day at the petrol station restroom became a cherished reminder that joy can be found in the most unexpected circumstances. It was a delightful lesson in embracing the unexpected and the absurd, making the most out of every situation, and finding humor even in the mundane moments of life on the road.

And so, as Angelo continued his truck driving adventures, he held onto the memory of that whimsical encounter, knowing that a simple playful response could turn an ordinary moment into a laugh-out-loud memory. The road ahead was filled with countless more adventures, but nothing could ever quite match the hilarity of that fateful day in the truck stop restroom. After all, life is a wild ride, and it's the unexpected pit stops that often leave us with the biggest smiles and the fondest memories.

CHAPTER 8 My absolutely beautiful wife

A British lady married an Italian man many years ago. The couple, after living in London for a few years, decided to move to Rome, the place where Christian, the husband, grew up. They are enjoying the warm weather; they love going on hikes and spend most of their time in nature.

Christian is very proud of his wife and never fails to let her know how beautiful she is; he tells her that every day. One day he decided to take the train to visit his brother, who lives in Florence.

While on the train, he sits next to a younger man who seems to have an English accent, and Christian starts the conversation by explaining that his wife is also British.

The two men talked for a while, and the young man asked, "How did you meet your wife?"

"I met her many years ago in a coffee shop. I was working there, and she was a customer. It was love at first sight; she was absolutely beautiful..."

"Oh, that sounds nice... do you have a picture of her?"

Christian, very happy that the young man asked, pulls out his phone and shows the guy a few pictures of his wife over the years and said, "She is beautiful, isn't she?"

The guy was confused and asked, "If you think your wife is good-looking, you should see my girlfriend."

"Is she that beautiful?"

"No," the young man chuckled, "she is an ophthalmologist."

Christian was taken aback for a moment but then realized what the young man meant. He laughed heartily and said, "Oh, I see! You meant she has a good eye for beauty as an ophthalmologist! That's a clever one!"

The two continued to chat and share stories throughout the train journey, finding common interests and enjoying each other's company. Christian couldn't help but appreciate the young man's witty sense of humor, and they soon became good travel companions.

As they arrived in Florence, Christian bid farewell to his new friend, grateful for the unexpected encounter. He couldn't wait to share this amusing story with his wife when he got back home.

Back in Rome, Christian reunited with his wife and recounted the train journey, including the humorous exchange with the young man. They both laughed heartily, cherishing yet another shared memory of joy and laughter. From that day on, Christian always looked back on that train journey with fondness. It was a reminder of how humor and light-heartedness can brighten even the simplest moments in life. And in the beauty of their love and adventures, Christian and his wife continued to create cherished memories together, embracing each day with laughter, love, and an appreciation for life's delightful surprises.

CHAPTER 9 Dinner with Alfred

Two men in their sixties regularly meet every weekend to watch football together. They are both Manchester United fans and it has been a ritual for them to watch the game together since they were teenagers. They met when they were kids and they have been close since.

One day Richard and his wife Kayla decide to invite his friend Alfred and his wife over for dinner. Alfred accepts happily.

They spend a very nice time at dinner enjoying the meal and the good company. After dinner, the wives go to the kitchen while the husbands stay at the table talking to each other. Alfred says:" A few days ago we went out to eat at the new restaurant just a few blocks away. It was amazing! I have not eaten so well in years… you should go!"

Richard asks:" Oh really? What is the name of the restaurant"?

Alfred goes silent, it seems like he cannot remember it and then he said: "What is the name of that flower that you give to someone you love? You know…the red one…"

"…the rose?"

"Yes" shouts Alfred and then he says "Roseeee, what is the name of the restaurant we went to the other day?"

Richard and Alfred share a hearty laugh, both amused and touched by the charming way Alfred asked for help to remember. It is a testament to the enduring friendship they share, where they can find joy even in the moments that highlight the passage of time.

As they finally remember the name of the restaurant, they continue to chat, reminiscing about their younger days and how much has changed since they first met. They toast to their lifelong friendship and the memories they've created together. When the wives return with dessert and coffee, they find Richard and Alfred still immersed in conversation, the glint of friendship shining in their eyes. The rest of the evening is filled with more laughter, more stories, and more cherished moments shared between two old friends who have stood the test of time.

As the night draws to a close, Richard and Alfred say their goodbyes, promising to meet again soon for another football match. Their bond remains as strong as ever, a testament to the enduring power of friendship, love, and shared passions that continue to bring them together, weekend after weekend, year after year.

CHAPTER 10 What a terrible day!

Olivia and Emma, two divorced ladies in their seventies, had once been starry-eyed romantics with hopes of meeting their soulmates. But as the years passed, they became less and less positive about their dating lives. Life had its twists and turns, and despite both getting married at some point, their marriages did not work out as they had hoped.

Olivia was known for her patience, shyness, soft-spoken nature, and her unwavering positivity and sweetness. On the other hand, Emma was the complete opposite - impulsive, always complaining, and often in a bad-temper. However, she had a way of making Olivia laugh, and they formed an unbreakable bond as friends.

One sunny day, Olivia was supposed to meet Emma at the park for their routine iced coffee date. As she climbed the stairs to get to the meeting spot, an unfortunate accident occurred, and Olivia slipped, resulting in a broken ankle. Despite the pain, when Emma later rushed to the hospital, she found Olivia laughing and chatting with the nurse as if nothing had happened.

Concerned for her friend, Emma rushed to Olivia's side, asking what happened. Olivia reassured her, "Nothing to worry about. I broke my ankle, but it will be okay." Emma couldn't help but feel relieved at her friend's positive attitude despite the circumstances.

Curious about the accident, Emma asked, "How did you do it?"

Olivia's laughter bubbled forth as she replied, "Oh, I'm just getting old, and I couldn't even walk up the stairs properly." She continued to share light-hearted jokes about her clumsy moment, making Emma chuckle alongside her.

After a moment of light-heartedness, Emma felt the need to share her own struggles of the day. "Oh, do not ask. I had a terrible day too."

Concerned, Olivia inquired, "What happened?"

With a sigh, Emma started, "My former sister-in-law called me to tell me that my ex-husband got hit by a bus today."

Olivia's face contorted in shock, "Oh, that is terrible. I'm so sorry to hear that."

Emma went on, "And on top of that, my boss also called me and told me that I got fired."

Olivia's eyes widened in surprise, "You were still working? You didn't mention that to me."

"I just started last week, and it was part-time," Emma explained.

Curious, Olivia asked, "What job were you doing?"

Emma's reply left Olivia momentarily speechless, "I was a bus driver... or at least I was until this afternoon."

The absurdity of the situation hit Olivia, and she couldn't help but chuckle, "Oh, Emma, only you could end up with such a bizarre twist of fate."

Emma shrugged with a grin, "Well, I guess I won't be driving buses anytime soon. But you know what, I'll find something else. Life always has a way of surprising us."

Olivia admired her friend's resilience, "You're right, Emma. Life may throw us curveballs, but as long as we have each other, we'll make it through. We may not have found our soulmates, but we found an incredible friendship that's worth its weight in gold."

Emma nodded with a smile, "Absolutely, Olivia. We may not have found love in the traditional sense, but our friendship is a love that sustains us through both the highs and lows of life."

As the two friends continued to chat and share stories, they both knew that no matter what challenges life threw at them, they would always have each other to lean on. In the company of a true friend, the burden of life's hardships felt a little lighter, and the moments of joy felt a little sweeter. And so, Olivia and Emma embraced the unpredictability of life, knowing that together, they could face anything that came their way, with laughter, support, and the strength of their enduring friendship.

CHAPTER 11 Widows and Dogs

In 1970, USA, in one village, several husbands had regretfully passed away because of the war or old age. There were a lot of widowed women, who occasionally felt lonely and depressed after losing their beloved husbands to death. Without their loving presence beside them, they felt a profound sense of sadness. Amidst this backdrop, a young woman from the middle class had a heartfelt idea. She decided to plan a local festival where dogs looking for owners would be on display. She had learned the value of dogs as devoted companions from reading numerous articles, and she believed they might be the ideal choice for many women in the village.

The idea was wonderful, and because the women in the town adored dogs, they all eagerly participated in the festival and purchased a dog to call their own. The dogs quickly became the widowed women's devoted companions ever after. They brought a new sense of joy and companionship to their lives, always there to keep each other company by strolling to the park together or cuddling on the couch while watching a movie. The presence of these loyal canine friends lessened their loneliness and brought a new warmth to their homes.

The widowed women learned valuable life lessons from their canine companions. They observed how dogs lived in the present moment, showing unconditional love, and appreciating even the little things in life. In fact, dogs became an amazing example of living life to the fullest and being genuinely happy with the simplest of pleasures. Since they got their dogs, the women seemed to have found a new sense of joy in their lives. They were no longer burdened by loneliness, thanks to the presence of their cute and loving dogs.

These faithful animals taught them that love and friendship could come from the most unlikely places and that spending time with a loyal dog could bring immense happiness within.

As the story of the widowed women and their dogs spread through the village, it became a source of inspiration and hope. The entire community learned the value of showing one another love and friendship because even the smallest act of kindness may have a big impact on the life of someone else. The village became a more caring and compassionate place as people realized the importance of supporting each other, especially in times of loss and hardship.

Over the years, the festival of dogs looking for owners became a cherished annual tradition in the village. It not only brought new companionship to widowed women but also created a sense of togetherness and community spirit among the villagers. The love and happiness shared between the women and their dogs were a testament to the power of human-animal connections and the profound impact they can have on one's life. The village thrived with love and friendship, guided by the heartwarming lesson that had begun with a simple idea to bring joy to a group of widowed women and their furry companions.

CHAPTER 12 Super Grandad

It is 9 pm. It is football night. On Tv, there is a Champions League match. Grandad Mo is a massive football fan. He used to play football when he was young but then he kept having back problems and had to stop. Slowly over the years, his back got worse and worse up to the point that now he cannot stand for too long.

He is watching the game with his grandkids. They are twins, and they love football too. They are 7 years old.

They are all excited to watch the game and hope the team they support wins the game.

Towards the end of the game, Grandad notices that the twins are very quiet, so he turns and notices that they are both sleeping.

After the game, he does not want to wake them up, but he does not want them to sleep on the sofa as it is not as comfortable as the bed. So, he carries them to the bedroom. Despite his bad back, the love for his grandkids makes him do what seemed to be impossible.

After tucking the twins gently into their cozy beds, Grandad Mo stands by their side for a moment, admiring their peaceful faces. He remembers the times when he used to play football with them in the backyard, their laughter echoing through the air. Those cherished memories fill his heart with warmth and gratitude, reminding him of the joy that his grandkids bring into his life.

As he slowly makes his way back to the living room, he can't help but think about how quickly time flies. It feels like just yesterday that his own children were the same age as these little ones, and now he's blessed with the joy of being a grandparent. Though his back still aches from the effort of carrying the twins, the love and happiness he feels overshadow any discomfort. For Grandad Mo, seeing his grandkids content and at peace is the greatest reward. He knows that these moments, spent together watching football, laughing, and making memories, are the ones that will remain etched in their hearts forever.

As he settles back into his favorite armchair, he glances at the clock and realizes that it's quite late. But he doesn't mind at all; the joy of spending time with his grandkids is worth every moment.

The next morning, Grandad Mo wakes up early to the sound of giggles and laughter coming from the twins' room. They are excitedly recounting the goals and moments from the game, not realizing that they had dozed off before it ended. Grandad chuckles to himself, thankful for the chance to witness these little miracles every day. Despite his back pain, Grandad Mo remains devoted to making special memories with his grandkids. He may not be able to run on the field like he used to, but he knows that the love and passion for football run strong in his family.

Throughout the day, the twins talk non-stop about the match, their enthusiasm contagious. Grandad listens intently, taking in every detail and sharing in their joy. He knows that these shared moments of football fandom will forever bond them as a family.

As the day unfolds, Grandad Mo decides to teach the twins a few football tricks that he learned during his playing days. With patience and a hint of nostalgia, he shows them how to kick the ball and dribble with finesse. The twins hang on to every word, their eyes shining with admiration for their grandad. Though his back may prevent him from playing the game physically, he finds a way to pass down his love for football to the next generation. Through these simple but heartfelt interactions, he feels a profound sense of fulfillment and purpose.

And so, the days go on, and Grandad Mo continues to be their biggest fan, both on and off the field. Together, they share the love for football that transcends generations, creating an unbreakable bond that will endure through time. In the embrace of family, the joy of the game, and the magic of love, Grandad Mo finds that life's most treasured moments are the ones spent with those who matter most.

CHAPTER 13 The Frozen Man

Kevin is a man in his fifties. He is always full of life, and he always has a smile on his face. He arrives in Heaven with the same attitude and energy. There are billions of people there at different times and with different stories. As he walks around to find some of the people he knew in life.

He sees his dad, grandparents, and some other people he knew there. He starts talking to them and having a good time.

After a while, he notices a man that seems completely cold, and it looks like he is almost frozen. So, he walks towards him and asks:

"Hey, are you ok?"

"Yes, I am okay," says the man while shivering.

"What did you die of? You seem very young; you must be in your thirties."

"I froze to death."

"How did that happen?"

"It is a long story...how did you die?"

"I died of joy!"

"How can someone die of joy?"

"I came home early after work, and I was sure that my wife was cheating on me. I had a vibe and sadly things were not great between us anymore. I started sprinting around the house looking for the guy she cheated on me with. I searched everywhere... in the garden, under the bed, in the wardrobe, in the bathroom, in the garage, in the kitchen... I didn't find anything. I was so relieved that my wife was not cheating that I died of joy!"

"Idiot, if you only searched in the freezer, we would both be alive..."

CHAPTER 14 "…and they lived happily ever after"

Mr. Turner, an English teacher, has eyes only for Miss Miller, a history professor, a sad and lonely woman who never smiles. She is very insecure; she believes nobody likes her, and she struggles to show affection towards other people. She never experienced love in any sort of relationship.

Turner, on the other hand, loves her from the first moment he sees her, but he is scared to approach her. He used to tell his friends, "You always have to try," "if you do not try, you will regret it," "She could be the one, just start a conversation" … and so on. However, after many years of rejection, he slowly lost hope in finding a woman. So, instead of approaching her and starting a conversation, he decides to use his main strength: writing.

He spent days and nights writing short poems for Miss Miller, but none of them seemed good enough. He wanted his words to convey the depth of his feelings for her, but every attempt felt inadequate. Eventually, after weeks of dedication and creativity, he finally wrote what he considered the best possible poem he could do.

After careful consideration, he decides to put his masterpiece in Miss Miller's locker. Then he sits at the table in the staff room, anxiously waiting for her to see it. The moments seem to stretch on forever as he nervously glances at the clock. Finally, he spots Miss Miller approaching her locker. His heart pounds in his chest as she retrieves the poem, her expression unreadable.

She reads the poem quietly, her eyes scanning each carefully chosen word. As she finishes, a soft blush spreads across her cheeks. She turns and looks at him with a big smile, a smile that he had never seen before. She looks super happy and flattered, and her transformation is mesmerizing. She shyly walks towards him, and the room seems to fade away as they lock eyes. She says, "This is such a beautiful poem! And yes...to reply to your question, I would love to go out with you."

Mr. Turner cannot believe it. He finally gets to go on a date with the girl he has always had a crush on. He is truly joyful, his heart bursting with happiness and excitement.

They went out the following day, and their connection only deepens with every moment they spend together. Miss Miller opens up to him, sharing her fears and insecurities, and he listens attentively, providing comfort and support. Through their conversations, they discover how much they have in common, their shared passion for teaching, literature, and history, creating an unbreakable bond between them.

As days turn into weeks and weeks into months, they become inseparable. Miss Miller is a changed woman, showing up at work with a smile from ear to ear. The once sad and lonely woman now radiates happiness and confidence, all thanks to the love and understanding of Mr. Turner.

In turn, Mr. Turner gains confidence in himself, knowing that he is capable of winning the heart of such an amazing woman. He starts working out, not to impress anyone, but to be the best version of himself for her and their future together.

Their love blossoms, and their relationship grows stronger with each passing day. After a few months, they decide to take the next step in their journey together. They get married in a beautiful ceremony surrounded by friends and family who see the genuine happiness in their eyes. Soon after, they welcome their children into the world, Laureen and Leon, who become the joy and light of their lives. Mr. Turner and Miss Miller cherish every moment of parenthood, passing down their love for learning, history, and the beauty of life to their little ones.

Their love story becomes a legend among their colleagues and students, a heartwarming tale of how love can heal and transform even the most broken hearts. Together, Mr. Turner and Miss Miller continue to inspire others with their unwavering love, compassion, and dedication to each other and their family. And so, their love story endures, like a beautiful poem written in the stars, a testament to the power of love, hope, and second chances. Their hearts forever entwined, they walk hand in hand, embracing the adventure of life together, writing a new chapter every day, and cherishing the profound love that brought them together against all odds.

CHAPTER 15 The thief

A burglar enters a house with a gun and finds a man and a woman passionately kissing. He ties up the woman and threatens the man to kill him if he does anything.

The man says, "Take whatever you want, but let her go."

Then the thief replies: "Do you love your wife so much?"

"This is the neighbor; my wife will be home soon."

CHAPTER 16 Penguins and Seals

There once was a penguin by the name of Dixie. Dixie and his family were residents of Antarctica. One day, unintentionally lost his family during a snowstorm. He was terrified and depressed, but Dixie persevered. He decided to scour Antarctica in search of his family. During his search he saw in the distance some animals he could not quite understand what they were. As he got closer, he asked them "Hey, I have never seen you around. What animal are you?"

"We are seals, my friend" one of the seals replied, sounding extremely friendly. Dixie asked them if he saw his family, explaining to them he lost them in a snowstorm and wondered if those seals had seen them. One of the seals told him he saw some penguins and guided him in the right direction along the way. Dixie observed numerous other polar animals as they traveled across vast ice fields. Eventually, thanks to the help of those seals Dixie finally found his family after days of looking. Everyone was ecstatic to see one another once more! Paul recognized the value of family and the need to fight for what one cares about, no matter the odds.

CHAPTER 17 Childbirth

It's 10 pm when a pregnant lady is in her living room with her husband watching TV. Suddenly, the lady starts panicking as she feels like her waters have broken. The husband rushes to help her to get in the car and they go to the hospital. Fortunately, they arrived at the hospital in just a few minutes and the doctors helped her straight away.

A group of nurses helps her to lie in a bed and she is being carried with her to the delivery room.

The doctor begins to tell her to push...but the light goes out...blackout! Panic.

A candle is lit to enable the doctor to continue his work while they hope to have the light back on. After a minute he says "So good, a beautiful baby man! "She cries tears of joy,

The doctor exclaims again:" Oh, another one! It's a female" and the new mom is very happy to hear that.

The doctor: "...another baby?!?" sounding very surprised by it.

And he blows out the candle.

The woman shouts: "What are you doing?!"

and the doctor says, "The light attracts them!"

CHAPTER 18 The Wife

It is a cold night in December. Jack and Patrick work as truck drivers and they are driving the whole night. They have known each other for a few years and always love spending time bantering and having fun. They used to hang out a lot as teenagers but as they both got a job and got married their lifestyle completely changed.

They meet up after work sometimes, often with her wives as the four of them get along very well.

After a few hours of driving, they need a quick break. They stop at a motorway rest stop to go to the bathroom. After a few minutes, the first one left the bathroom and lit one cigarette.

As he is ready to hit the road again, he looks for his friend but cannot find Impatiently he comes back to the toilet and sees him still looking in his pants.

"So, what are you doing? You have been there for ages".

"I know… every time my wife puts her hands on something you can never find anything!"

CHAPTER 19 Looking at the Bright Side

In a small village in Norway, there is a group of swimmers. They are all together in this small village away from the distraction of the world. They are professional and they decided to move her for a few months to fully focus on training and become better athletes.

Every day they wake up, have practice in the morning for a couple of hours, then they go to the gym for an hour. After that, they have lunch and rest till evening when they do another training session. It is very hard, some of them quit after a few weeks. It is guys between the age of 19 and 30 and most of them have girlfriends, family, and wives away from them and live in a place that does not offer many distractions.

One of them is extremely dedicated, he is 24 years old, he wants to compete at the highest levels and plans his diet, training, and rest since he was 14. He seems to be the only one enjoying the time there. He is excited at the fact that he can get better every day, everything is being paid for, there are good coaches and there are no distractions.

His teammates admire his stoic mentality, but question how he can be that happy in such challenging conditions. They ask "Hey, how can you always be so happy? We love training and getting better, but in this place there is nothing else to do and the coaches can get very mad at us for no specific reason".

The guy replied "Yeah..." and then added "But we can train every day and we do not have anything else to worry about".

"What do you mean "nothing else to worry about"?

"I was not a pro up until a few months ago, I had to work part-time to pay the bills. Here I don't have to do that. I am getting paid enough".

"Yeah, but it is not a lot of money".

"True, but we can get better and earn more money in the future by becoming better swimmers".

"...the coaches scream at us for no reason, they are too hard on us. It feels like it is a jail".

"True, some of them are very harsh, but it is good for me to develop a stronger mentality".

They kept discussing it and sharing their past experiences and point of view.

Then another guy says "Gosh, I miss my family so much! I cannot wait to hug my wife" and then looked at the guy and said, "what about you, do you miss your girl?"

"I do...a lot".

"Oh, so there is something that makes you sad" and they laughed.

"Well, I miss her a lot, but I strongly believe distance will make us stronger, so it is all good".

Moral of the story: A situation is rarely completely negative; it is all about the perception.

CHAPTER 20 "60 Years Anniversary"

Mason and Karen, an elderly couple, were the envy of the entire village due to their extraordinary bond. Throughout their lives, they had been known for their unique personalities, and together, they created an aura of joy and love that was simply contagious. Mason was hailed as the village comedian, with his infectious sense of humor, unwavering positivity, and a heart full of altruism. His friends could always count on him to lift their spirits and make them laugh, even during the toughest of times. Karen, on the other hand, was the epitome of politeness, with a penchant for compliments from her beloved husband. She had been a vibrant and fun-loving woman in her youth, especially during her teenage years when she used to take dance lessons and practice her moves at home. But as age caught up with her, her energy waned, though her spirit remained as lively as ever.

This weekend marked the anniversary of their very first date, a momentous occasion that the couple cherished dearly. Exactly 60 years ago, Mason had mustered the courage to ask Karen out for a romantic walk by the lake, setting the stage for a lifetime of love and laughter.

To celebrate this remarkable milestone, Mason planned a special dinner for the two of them at an upscale restaurant in a nearby city. The table was adorned with flowers and candles, creating the perfect ambiance for a romantic date. As they sat together, reminiscing about the past and sharing jokes, they seemed to have recaptured the magic of being a young couple in their twenties.

Curiosity got the better of Karen, and she playfully asked, "Did you fall in love with me at first sight, Mason?"

He chuckled and replied, "I've told you this a million times, my dear. It wasn't love at first sight, but I definitely felt something extraordinary. My love for you grew day by day, and each passing moment with you only deepened my affection."

She looked at him with fondness and inquired, "What was it about me that made you fall in love?"

Mason's eyes sparkled as he recollected the memories of their youth. "Oh, Karen, it was many things that captured my heart - your infectious laughter, the way your eyes lit up when you spoke about your passions, your kindness towards everyone you met, and your adventurous spirit that danced with joy. But above all, it was your ability to make even the most mundane moments feel extraordinary."

Flattered by his words, Karen blushed and playfully teased him, "Tell me honestly, do you prefer rich or intelligent women?"

Mason's response was swift and full of love, "Neither, my dear. I adore you just the way you are, with your unique blend of kindness, wit, and charm. Your genuine self is what has always captured my heart."

As the night continued, they laughed, danced, and shared more beautiful memories from their journey together. The love that had blossomed over the past six decades showed no sign of waning, and they reveled in each other's company as if they were still two young hearts embarking on a magical adventure. For Mason and Karen, every moment was a celebration of their love, and with each passing year, their bond grew stronger, proving that true love knows no boundaries of age or time. In their love-filled world, the joy of togetherness would always reign supreme, and their unique connection would continue to inspire those around them for generations to come.

CHAPTER 21 Peter and the Professor

When Peter was studying law at the University of Luton, he had a professor who couldn't stand him.

Peter, however, was not one to be intimidated. One day Professor Mason was eating in the school cafeteria and Peter decided to sit next to him.

The professor said: "Peter, do you know that a pig and a bird cannot eat together?"

"Okay Mr. Mason, but I'm flying away regardless" was Peter's answer before he got up and moved to another table.

The professor was very annoyed and decided to take revenge by making Peter do a surprise exam.

However, Peter is always prepared and answered all questions brilliantly.

The professor understood that Peter was prepared and thought of another way of trying to embarrass him. So, when it looked like he did not have more questions he asked: "What would you do if you were given the choice to have wisdom or a big quantity of money?"

"Certainly money," replied Peter.

"Ah…that is silly" replied the professor and added "I would have chosen wisdom in your place. As wisdom is the cornerstone of any type of success. Financial one too"

"You are right Professor…we all choose what we do not have."

The Professor was fuming at Peter's lack of respect and arrogance. He asked his student for the notebook to mark the surprise exam and wrote in capital letters "IDIOT" and closed the notebook.

Peter took it and walked away. As he was walking away, he wanted to check what the mark was, so he opened the notebook. When he saw the "IDIOT" in capital letters he said: "Professor, I noticed that you signed the exam, but you forgot to mark it" while showing it to the class.

The class burst into laughter and the professor was super upset.

CHAPTER 22 Christmas Tree

It is the beginning of December, and on the streets of Montreal, it is possible to see Christmas lights, and in the houses, people are decorating Christmas trees.

Callum is a little boy that loves Christmas and asked his parents for one. Unfortunately, his parents are struggling financially and cannot afford to buy it. As days go by and the 25th of December is getting closer, the parents can see that their son is getting sad that he does not have a Christmas tree, unlike his friends.

The parents want their son to be happy, so they decide to cut some expenses and make some sacrifices to afford the tree for their son.

So, one day the mom says: "Callum, ask your dad where he is going?"

Callum asked "Daddy, where are you going?"

"I am going to make you happy, when I will be back you will understand" replied his dad.

"Why are you taking that weapon with you?" asked the son that seemed very intrigued by that object.

The dad started laughing and said, "This is a woodcutter's axe."

"What's it for? Please Daddy tells me! Are you going to get a tree for me?" said Callum showing a lot of enthusiasm.

"Okay, I'm going out now, and when I come back, I'll have a wonderful Christmas tree with me" replied the dad while putting on a heavy overcoat and snow boots.

The son was jumping around the house radiating joy. 5 minutes later the dad comes back home with an amazing Christmas tree, the most beautiful

Callum has ever seen.

Callum started screaming out of joy and hugging his dad and then said: "Dad, how did you cut a tree so quickly?"

The dad honestly replied: "I didn't cut the tree, I got it at the supermarket down the road."

"At the supermarket?" asked Callum

"Yes," the dad replied.

"Why did you bring that axe with you then?"

"Oh Callum, I needed this to avoid paying for the tree".

CHAPTER 23 Duration of calls

Man to man: 00:00:39

Two buddies are on the phone, and as soon as they connect, they go into full "guy mode." They start talking about sports, burgers, and their latest "manly" exploits. They even have a competition to see who can finish a burrito the fastest while still talking. The time flies, and they end the call with a burp and a fist bump, declaring themselves the kings of manly conversations.

Son calls Mom: 00:00:47

The son calls his mom, and the moment she picks up, he launches into the classic "mom update mode." He tells her about his day, every meal he's eaten, and even how he finally managed to do his laundry. He knows he's got to be quick before she starts telling him how to fold his socks properly. By the end of the call, his mom has already planned a week's worth of meals for him, and he's trying to figure out how to decline politely without hurting her feelings.

Son calls Dad: 00:00:29

The son calls his dad, but there's a catch – his dad is known for his super brief answers. "Hey, Dad, how's it going?" the son asks. "Good," comes the reply. "Did you catch the game last night?" the son tries again. "Yep," says his dad. It's a challenge to have a full conversation, but the son is determined. He ends up playing 20 questions with his dad just to get a few more words out of him. Success!

Man calls woman: 01:00:20

This poor guy is so nervous about calling the woman he likes that he's been practicing his "smooth" introduction for an hour. When she finally picks up, he forgets everything he rehearsed and ends up speaking like a cheesy romantic movie character. He tries to compliment her, but his brain is like a malfunctioning robot spouting cheesy lines. It's cringeworthy and hilarious, but surprisingly, she finds it adorable and can't stop laughing.

Woman calls woman: 08:29:59

When these two best friends get on the phone, they become unstoppable chatterboxes. They talk about everything from their latest crushes to their wildest dreams, and the conversation keeps going and going. They even start having a pretend argument about who can talk the fastest and end up laughing so hard they can barely breathe. They're practically creating their own language by the end of the call.

Man calls girlfriend: 01:12:13

The guy is so excited to talk to his girlfriend that he starts rambling about every single thought that crosses his mind. He tells her about the crazy dream he had last night, what he ate for breakfast, and even starts describing the squirrel he saw in the park. She patiently listens and can't help but giggle at his adorable enthusiasm. By the time he realizes how long he's been talking, he's convinced he's broken a world record for the longest monologue.

Woman calls boyfriend: 06:14:29

When the woman calls her boyfriend, they both get so lost in the conversation that they forget about the outside world. They talk about everything from their favorite movies to their secret talents, and they're having so much fun that they don't even notice the hours flying by. They even start making up silly songs together and end up with a hilarious duet that should probably never be recorded.

Husband calls wife: 00:00:06

The husband dials his wife's number, and before he can even say a word, she answers with an enthusiastic, "Hey, honey!" He's amazed by her psychic skills, jokingly asking if she has a crystal ball to predict his calls. She giggles and says she just knows when her "hubby senses" are tingling. It's a brief but sweet conversation filled with inside jokes and plenty of laughter.

Wife calls husband: 19 unanswered calls

The wife calls her husband, but it seems like he's on an adventure in the Bermuda Triangle because he's mysteriously unreachable. She starts leaving increasingly funny voicemails, pretending to be the president or an alien trying to make contact. After 19 unanswered calls, she finally gets through to him and says, "Hey, did you just escape Area 51? I've been trying to reach you for ages!" They both burst into laughter, and he promises to check his phone more often, just in case she's calling from outer space.

In the hilarious world of phone calls, laughter is the universal language. From awkward moments to playful banter, each conversation is a delightful journey filled with joy and connection. And no matter how long or short the call, one thing's for sure – it's the laughter that keeps hearts warm and spirits high!

CHAPTER 24 The Life of Andrew

Andrew is a young man with the dream of becoming a famous drummer. He is playing with his band this week as they have a small concert. His performance is poor, it is one of those days…his friends are upset and disappointed with him and instead of driving home together, they leave him alone in the middle of nowhere. He started walking home, which was hundreds of miles away. He did not know where to go. He was just walking on the road that he thought he took with his friends to get to the beach.

While he was there, lonely, and sad he heard music and cheering from not far. As it is getting late, and he does not have anywhere to sleep he decides to go there hoping to find a place where to sleep. As he gets there, he sees a girl from a distance, she is blonde, quite short with a bright smile. He is normally a good-looking and confident man, but this time he does not feel confident enough to go and talk to the girl as he has not showered in a long time and has not eaten in hours.

However, the girl smiles at him and slowly makes her way toward him, and says: "Hey, you look lost, are you okay?"

Andrew was embarrassed at the idea that the girl he liked approached him only to let him know that he looks lost. He then replies: "Yeah, long story…I am looking for a place to sleep tonight. Do you know any place nearby?"

They started talking and she helped him to find a place to sleep. Over the following weeks, they start dating and eventually, he finds out that her dad is a famous musician.

The daughter helps her boyfriend set up an appointment with her dad. The two talk for a while, and her dad sees potential in him. He not only admires Andrew's passion for music but also sees the determination in his eyes. Impressed, he decides to lend a helping hand to this young, struggling musician. With her dad's guidance and support, Andrew gets an opportunity to audition for a big band and finally achieve his dream. His drumming skills are appreciated, and he is offered a spot in the band, launching him into the world of fame and success.

The moral of the story: do not get disappointed because of a bad day. Nothing happened without a reason. Sometimes, the most unexpected encounters can lead to life-changing opportunities. And as Andrew looks back on that fateful night when he was left stranded, he realizes that it was the start of a beautiful journey that brought him not only his dream career but also the love of his life.

CHAPTER 25 "I felt like I was a famous footballer…"

Mike is a Dutch man in his thirties. He is very serious about his job and very funny around his friends. It is like two different people. He is a lawyer, and he is quite a successful one.

After working for most of the year he gives him and his girlfriend a holiday in Lake Como and Rome. They have never been to Italy before and after listening to their friends' experiences in Italy they decided to book a flight and visit two beautiful places: Lake Como, known for its stunning views, and Rome, rich in history in every corner.

After enjoying the holiday for a couple of weeks they go back to Amsterdam.

As soon as Mike returned to the city, he told his friends: "You can't understand what happened to me! Yesterday, on my way back from Rome, I got off the plane and…". His voice trembling with emotion, he looks emotional and can't continue the story.

His friends encourage him: "Did you get off the plane and… what happened?"

Mike seems unable to continue his story and his friends start to get worried as they imagine something happened to their friend.

Eventually, he says: "I got off the plane and there were thousands of people there for me! People cheering me, with banners written in various languages, all there just for me! People of any age and gender were singing, clapping their hands, and throwing kisses at me… I felt like a famous footballer coming back home after winning the World Cup!"

His friends listen to Mike, but they do not believe what he is saying. They think he is joking, but Mike insists that he is being serious. His friends start laughing at him telling him that he must have been dreaming or that he must have taken some drugs. Mike tried his best to tell them he experienced that and eventually said: "Look if you don't believe me, you can ask the Pope who was with me at that moment, and he saw everything!!!".

CHAPTER 26 "Do you have Tomato Ice cream?"

Pamela and Bruce are two extremely busy parents that work their 9 to 5, and, in the evening, Bruce works on his side hustles to make a bigger income and provide for his family, while Pamela looks after their kid, Jamie. Jamie is a very hyperactive kid who loves to play like every 7 years old kid.

It is summer and Pamela and Bruce feel like they need some time for themselves as a couple and book a holiday to go to Greece. Pamela's dad, Grandpa Henry, is going to look after Jamie for the week.

Henry is very excited to spend time with his grandkid and the first day they go to watch a football game.

On their way back home, they walk past an ice cream shop and Jamie wants to go in. As they step in the kid asks the man working behind the counter:" Do you have the tomato flavour?"

The counter starts laughing and says kindly "No we do not" while smiling at their grandad for the weird request the kid made.

Every day they go in and the kid always asks for the same flavour.

The following week the kid sneaks out of the house to meet his friends to go to the shop and asks again "Do you have tomato flavours?"

"Dear children, I already told you no". The ice cream man replies a bit annoyed, and the children leave while laughing.

The following day the same thing happens, and the ice cream man says: "If you ask me again, I'll make a tiger bite your butt" The ice cream man shouts impatiently, and the children run away.

The following day, the children enter the ice cream shop again: "Hello, do you have a tiger?".

Ice cream man: "No!"

The children: "So do you have tomato ice cream?"

CHAPTER 27 "I would like the pink, the brown and the red one".

A beautiful lady of about thirty-five divorced a few years back. Since then, she never wanted to know about men. Her friends try to push her to "go back out there" as her best friend Lily used to tell her every single time they go out. However, she lost hope to find a good man to be with. Years go by and her friends wonder what the last time she had an intimate relationship with a man.

She tells them that it has been years, leaving her friends speechless and shocked at the news.

They try to talk to her and tell her that it would be good for her to go on dates and get to know other people, even just platonically.

She realized that her friends have a good point and so she decides to sign up on a dating app. Weeks go by and she starts texting a man that she seems to get along with. She eventually goes out with him and the two of them seem to have a special chemistry. They keep seeing each other for a while but sadly the man stops texting her and seems nowhere to be found. She feels very sad about it, and she convinces herself that no good man exists.

One day while watching a romantic movie she decides to go to a small shop, approaches the clerk, and asks him for a vibrator.

The clerk shows her all the options they have and invites her to choose discreetly and walks away.

The lady looks at them one by one and she calls the clerk.

"I decided," she says.

"Please tell me, ma'am".

"I would like the pink one on the left, the brown one up there, and the red one."

"For the pink and brown ones, no problem... but dear lady, the fire extinguisher is not for sale".

CHAPTER 28 Reunion

A group of people in their thirties go to eat together in a restaurant and then go to a bar where there is a reunion of people that went to the same school many years back. Among those hundreds of people, some five guys have not seen each other in a while, and they used to be in the same class in secondary school. They all had different ways of life and they lived in different cities and countries, so it was hard for them to meet up. Despite the difficulties to plan something they are finally able to meet.

The night is going great, they talk about each other's lives, some of them are married, others are singles; some of them still have the same lifestyle as teenagers, while others started to hate going out as they become older.

One of the guys approaches a woman at the club, she is very pretty, and he does not seem to remember her from school many years before. They start talking and they find out they went to the same school many years back but for some reason, they did not cross paths back then.

They leave the bar and go back to her place which is just a few blocks away. After a long night of making love, he notices a photo of another man on her bedside table and starts worrying.

The man starts asking who that guy is, but she does not answer and does not take the question seriously. The guy keeps asking wondering if the guy is a boyfriend or a relative. He is very confused and quite worried. He keeps asking and eventually, she says "That is me before becoming a woman."

CHAPTER 29 The Joker

At 7 am a man returns to his house trying to make as little noise as possible. Unfortunately for him, waiting for him at the end of the corridor is his wife, very angry!

"Good morning The Joker, don't you think you're a little late??!" she yells at him.

"Wait dear, I can explain everything to you! I've been with that client I was telling you about."

"Oh, yes? And you worked with him all night? Really? she retorted.

"But I told you it was a very important thing, a deal I couldn't let go of... so after finding an agreement I took him to dinner in a nice restaurant."

"And you were there until 7 in the morning, The Joker? Do you think I'm stupid?"

"No, what are you saying? After that, it got late but he wanted to go to a pub to continue our business discussion and we stayed there until 3..."

"Ah really... you have been with him till 3 am... and after that what did you do, The Joker??"

"Afterwards we were driving home but his car didn't start so he asked me if I could give him a lift to his house which is on the other side of the city, so..."

"Listen, The Joker, stop it... am I supposed to believe all the lies you're telling me??"

"Let me explain..." the husband insisted and then paused for a second and said, "anyway why do you keep calling me The Joker?"

"Because only The Joker wears so much lipstick".

CHAPTER 30 Clarissa and Charlotte

In the villa of a noble family, they desperately need a maid to look after the huge mansion.

After weeks of interviewing the picky wife, Charlotte finally found a woman to hire. The girl, Miss Clarissa has great experience as a maid and was recommended by a friend of Charlotte.

After 4 months of working there, Clarissa told Charlotte she needed to talk to her, they had a brief conversation and then she asked:

"I would like to get a raise."

Charlotte was annoyed at the request and asked why she would give her a raise just after 4 months of work and on top of that, she was getting paid already quite well.

The maid said that she has not one, but four reasons for why she deserves a raise. Charlotte was shocked at her maid's request and asked her to elaborate.

Clarissa said:" First of all, I do my job extremely well. I do more than I am paid for…"

Charlotte did not reply as she recognized that Clarissa had a point. Then Clarissa added: "Secondly, I iron better than her!"

"That is funny! And why would you say that?"

"Do you believe your husband? Because that is what he told me" And then added "Thirdly, I am a better cook than you are. I prepare wonderful meals unlike you".

"Okay, now you are talking nonsense!" the lady shouted and then asked, "and did my husband tell you this too?"

"Yes, Ma'am… and lastly, I am a better lover than you are!"

"How dare you!!?? Did you sleep with my husband?? You are fired!"

"No, ma'am. Rodrigo, the driver, told me that".

"How much did you say you want as a raise dear?"

CHAPTER 31 "Sit down I said!"

It is a warm day of summer. Leon is a young recruit that is taking the bus going home, where his family is waiting for him for dinner.

The bus is quite busy, but he still finds a place to sit. After a few stops, a sergeant gets on the bus. There are no seats, so the sergeant stands, right in front of the recruit.

The recruit waves for him to get up, but the sergeant quickly tells him, "Be comfortable, boy. Stay there"

"Well, thank you sergeant, but I-"

"No buts," the sergeant interrupts him, "I said you can stay there" with an authoritative manner.

After a few minutes, the sergeant still has not found a seat. The young recruit again nods that he wants to stand up, but again the sergeant rejects the offer, "Sit down I said," he orders.

"Yes, sergeant but…" again tries to say to the recruit.

"I said sit!!!"

A few more minutes pass, and the recruit again tries to leave his seat, but the sergeant once again orders him to sit, because there was no need for him to leave his seat.

But at this point, the desperate recruit replies, "I understand that I have to sit, but I should have got off three stops ago! My parents are waiting for me for dinner!"

CHAPTER 32 Rebellious Teenager

Sarah is a rebellious teenager. Her parents are struggling with her. Even the smallest things seem to cause problems. She is very argumentative.

One morning her mom goes to the kitchen and finds a milk bottle opened without a lid on the table. So, she asked her daughter: "Honey, did you drink milk this morning?"

"Yes"

"So, could you please put it back in the fridge after using it? You always leave it open on the table".

"Whatever, it is the same thing."

"No, it is not… what do you think the refrigerator is for?!"

"Well, when there was no refrigerator, what did people use to do?"

CHAPTER 33 A Super-Intelligent Parrot

One day, Daniel, the owner of a super-intelligent parrot, must leave for a few days because he has an important international business meeting in Dubai. He blindly trusts the animal's intelligence and does not call anyone to look after his parrot as he believes its parrot is more intelligent than many of his friends.

So, he gives Parrott an assignment. On Wednesday he must order 5 loaves of bread so that when he is back home on Thursday, he will have fresh bread. Daniel set up his phone ready so that his parrot only must press one button and order 5 loaves of bread. The master, before leaving, repeats a thousand times to the parrot to be careful not to get the number wrong.

It is Wednesday and the parrot presses the button and orders the bread. Unfortunately, instead of 5, he orders 500 without even realizing it.

The following day the owner comes back home and sees a massive delivery on his doorstep. He steps towards it crossed and confused. As soon as he realizes the animal's mistake he becomes enraged. He yells at the little parrot, picks it up, and carries it down to the basement. He takes one wing and nails it to the door and does the same with the other wing.

Leaving the poor little animal alone in the dark cellar, attached to the door. The parrot begins to look around looking for a way out. He does not find anything and starts to lose up. Then he looks up above him and catches sight of the Vitruvian Man on the wall, a drawing made by Leonardo Da Vinci.

The animal, not knowing who it was, says: "Hey, who are you?"

"I am a Vitruvian man!" whispers the man.

"Ahh … how long have you been here crucified?"

"Eh … A long time … hundreds of years now." The man sighs disconsolately

The parrot says: "Excuse me Man, how many loaves of bread did you order?"

CHAPTER 34 "I want lasagne!"

Two old ladies are seated on a bench and start talking:

"It's been a while since the last time we met. How have you been?"

"Good, thank you. And your husband?"

"He sadly passed away three weeks ago."

"Oh, I am sorry to hear that. I did not know about it. How did it happen? Last I remember, he was completely fine."

"That day he wanted me to prepare lasagne for him. I checked if I had all the ingredients, but I did not have enough cheese. So, I told him I could not make lasagne and I would have prepared rice and chicken instead. He insisted that he wanted to eat lasagne."

The friend said, "Yes, I remember he was stubborn. When he had something in his mind, there was nothing that could change his mind."

To which the widow replied, "Exactly! He left the house to go and buy cheese, but as soon as he left, he had a heart attack and passed away."

The other one was shocked and said, "Oh poor you, you must have been going through a lot... what did you do?"

"What was I supposed to do? I prepared rice and chicken."

The two ladies burst into laughter, finding humor in the irony of the situation. They both knew how strong-willed the woman's late husband was, and it was just like him to be determined to have lasagne even when the situation seemed a bit impractical.

As they continued to reminisce about the late husband's quirks and idiosyncrasies, their laughter echoed in the park, drawing curious glances from passersby. But they didn't care; they were savoring the moment of joy and camaraderie, finding comfort in each other's company during a difficult time.

The bench they were sitting on had become a symbol of their enduring friendship, a place where they shared stories, laughter, and even tears. Throughout the years, they had weathered life's ups and downs together, supporting and cheering each other on.

And on that particular day, as the sun began to set, casting a warm glow on the park, the two old ladies found solace in laughter, reminding themselves that amidst sorrow and loss, there is still room for happiness and shared memories.

As the days went by, they continued to meet on that same bench, cherishing their friendship and finding strength in each other's presence. And while they missed their departed loved ones dearly, they knew that the bond they had created would endure, just like the laughter that echoed in the park that day.

CHAPTER 35 A tourist in London

A Chinese tourist arrives in London; as soon as he leaves the airport, he takes a cab towards the Airbnb to which he was headed. On the way, they pass by Buckingham Palace and the tourist asks:

"Wow, it is beautiful. Do you know how long ago it was made?"

The driver replies:" I am not sure, but I guess hundreds of years."

"And how long ago did it take you to build it?"

"I do not know but I guess a few years."

The Chinese man bursts into laughter and adds: "Ahahah, in China we would have built it in a few months" and keeps making fun of the fact that in China they would have built it in a much shorter time.

After a while, they pass by Tower Bridge and the tourist is very impressed by the beauty of the bridge and asks the driver a few questions about it. He also asked how long it took to make it and the cab driver replied that he was not sure, but it probably took many months.

The Chinese man burst into a laugh again making fun of the man and saying that in China it would take a few weeks to create that.

The British Driver is very annoyed at the arrogance and disrespect of the tourist, and he prefers not to say anything because he would lose his temper.

They are now silent in the car. The tourist is looking at his phone, while the driver turns on the music and he is silently driving.

Just when they are about to get to the destination, the tourist notices The British Museum and asks the driver the same question: "How long did it take you to build it?" The Cab driver replies: "I have no idea! I was here this morning, and it was not here.

CHAPTER 36 Long-Distance

Farrah and Jack are a very nice couple. They do not live together yet, but they plan to in the future. They both live in Amsterdam, and they love their life there. One day, Farrah gets offered a great job that pays more than double her actual job in Berlin. After discussing it for a while with Jack, they think that taking the job is the best thing to do, and they agree to be long-distance.

After a few days, she flies to Berlin. After less than a month, she receives a letter from her boyfriend, and very excited, she opens it. She is eagerly anticipating a romantic message from Jack. So, she lies on the bed, opens the letter, and starts reading it:

"Dear Farrah, I am truly sorry, but I can no longer stand this situation, and I think we should break up. Long-distance is too much for me. The distance between us is too great. I must admit that I have been unfaithful to you a few times since you left, and you do not deserve this. I'm sorry. I wish you all the best. You deserve better.

Please could you return the picture you kept of us? Jack."

The woman was utterly heartbroken and devastated. She couldn't believe what she was reading. Tears streamed down her cheeks as she tried to come to terms with the sudden end of their relationship. For a week, she cried and mourned the love she thought they had shared. Then, amidst her sorrow, Farrah's heart turned to the desire for revenge. She couldn't let Jack's hurtful actions go unnoticed. She wanted him to feel a fraction of the pain she was feeling. So, she came up with a plan to get back at him.

She found tens and tens of pictures of good-looking guys on the internet and printed them out. With a mix of determination and a touch of mischief, she put all the pictures in an envelope, along with Jack's photo, and added a note that said:

"Jack, forgive me, I can't remember who you are! Just keep your picture and send me back the others."

The act of putting together this envelope was a cathartic experience for Farrah. It was her way of taking back some control and finding humor amidst the heartbreak. As she sealed the envelope, she couldn't help but smile through her tears, imagining Jack's surprise when he received it. Though the pain of the breakup lingered, Farrah found solace in her little act of revenge. She knew that healing would take time, but she was determined to move forward and find happiness again, with or without Jack.

As days turned into weeks and weeks into months, Farrah's heart began to mend. She focused on her new job in Berlin, made new friends, and rediscovered her strength and independence. And in the process, she learned that revenge might have brought a momentary sense of satisfaction, but the true victory was in finding herself again.

As she reflected on her journey, Farrah realized that she was on a path of growth and self-discovery. She knew that one day, the hurt and betrayal would fade away, and she would emerge stronger and ready to embrace the love and happiness that life had in store for her. And with every step she took, she whispered to herself, "I am enough, and I deserve the best."

CHAPTER 37 Camping Trip

Carmen and Jessica are on a camping trip. They are sisters and because of their commitments and work during the year, they do not get many chances to see each other. So, once a year they leave their husbands and kids and spend a week together camping. They used to love it as kids. Carmen used to love waking up in nature, away from the noises of city life. She works as an Astronomer and loves nature and the sky. Jessica loves waking up without having to rush to prepare her kids for school. She works as a nurse; she loves looking after people and helping. Shortly after they have dinner, they enter the tent, tell each other stories, and go to sleep.

A few hours later, Jessica wakes up and wakes up her sister.

"Carmen, sorry to wake you, but …" talking as if she saw a ghost "we can see the sky?"

Carmen replies, "Oh yes, and I also see millions of stars." feeling confused and sleepy at her sister's exclamation. Then, she added, "Can we go back to sleep now?"

Jessica: "What!?!? What do you think happened?"

Carmen ponders for a few seconds as she does not understand what her sister is about. Then, she remembers that her sister might want to know something about the stars and then replies:

"From an astronomical point of view, that tells me that there are millions of galaxies and, potentially, billions of planets.

From the astrological point of view, I observe that Saturn is in the constellation Leo.

From a temporal point of view, I deduce that it is about 3.30 am.

70

From the meteorological point of view, I assume tomorrow is going to be a beautiful sunny day".

"Carmen! Are you crazy? Can't you see that our tent has been stolen!!!?"

CHAPTER 38 "What do you feed him?"

In southern America, Polo is an old man that moved from Austria to retire somewhere warmer and sunnier. He enjoys nature and animals and starts working as a farmer. Spending time with animals makes him feel less lonely and more loved. He treats his animals with love and tries to do the best for them to make sure they live their best life.

One day he throws a party and many people of the village come by his house to see all the animals he has and enjoy the day. One gentleman passes by and says, "Nice pig, what do you feed him?"

The farmer: "I give him mainly the leftovers. I eat a lot so sometimes I prepare something just for him too."

The gentleman: "You should be ashamed! I'm from animal welfare! 100 Euros fine! You should not give him leftovers! How would you feel if I feed you with pig leftovers...not nice right? Then why do you do that to him?" and walks away very upset.

Polo is confused as to why the man was so bothered by that. He takes great pride in taking care of his animals and gets offended when someone thinks the opposite.

A few minutes later another guy passes by and says, "Nice pig, what do you feed him?"

Polo to avoid problems says, "Cappuccino and croissant in the morning, noodles with meat sauce for lunch, and steak for dinner."

"You should be ashamed! 1000 Euro fine, I am from 'world hunger,' there are starving children in this city, and you give a pig these very expensive meals! That is unbelievable!" and walks away.

Just a few minutes later another gentleman says: "Nice pig, what are you feeding him?"

The farmer: "I give him 10 euros and he goes and buys himself whatever he wants!"

CHAPTER 39 Spoiled Kids

Thomas and his wife Helena decide to change their summer holiday. They are used to going to hotels with their kids as they find hotels very comfortable, and they feel like they enjoy the holiday more. However, they are starting to realize that their kids, Julia, and Matthew, 13 and 14, are becoming the typical spoiled kids and they seem to take many things for granted. Therefore, they decide to have a different holiday, by going camping for a week, in a place where the connection is poor, there are no restaurants, and they will have to sleep in a tent.

When the parents communicated the idea to the kids, Julia and Matthew did not like that at all. Matthew complained because that meant he could not use his PlayStation, while Julia complained because she did not like the fact of sleeping in a tent.

As they drove there, the atmosphere in the car was not great. The kids at the back were in silence and they both looked very unhappy. They had to spend a week without a mobile phone, laptop, iPad, and PlayStation and it felt like a punishment.

Once they got to the place, they tried to make their tent. Thomas and Helena stayed in a tent, while their kids were supposed to sleep in another tent just a few yards from them. The kids at first refused to make the tent and expected their parents to do it for them.

In the evening, when it was time to go to sleep, the kids, scared that they did not have anywhere to sleep, started crying and begging their parents for help. Thomas and Helena refused to help them, they wanted to teach their kids a lesson.

Eventually, the kids managed to make the tent and went to sleep.

the following day the kids seemed much more enthusiastic, they both liked sleeping in the tent and found it fun. Thomas' itinerary was full of activities. The location was wonderful, with lakes and beautiful views.

At the end of the week, the kids did not want to leave. The holiday was so useful for them to understand that life is more than just an iPad and PlayStation.

CHAPTER 40 Apple Seeds

The young man strolled through the city streets, his curiosity piqued when he spotted a guy standing on top of a truck full of apples, peeling away and throwing the pulp while carefully collecting the seeds in a bag. Intrigued, the boy approached him, "Hey, what are you doing? Are you just throwing away all those apples?"

Confidently, the man on the truck replied, "Yep, that's exactly what I'm doing! But don't you know that apple seeds develop intelligence?"

The boy's eyebrows shot up, "Intelligence from apple seeds? Seriously?"

The man nodded, "Absolutely! And you know what? I sell these magical seeds!"

"Wait, you sell them? How much do they cost?" the increasingly intrigued boy asked.

The man grinned mischievously, "Five euros each!"

Without hesitation, the young man exclaimed, "Alright! I'll take three!"

The man took the 15 euros and handed over the three precious seeds to the boy. The boy swallowed them one by one, and then he thought aloud, "Hmm, but with 15 euros, I could buy 15 kilograms of apples, peel them, and have so many more seeds."

And the man replied, "See that? You're already becoming smarter just by considering that!"

The young man burst into laughter, "You're right! Give me three more!"

With a twinkle in his eye, the man handed over three additional seeds. The boy ate them with gusto, fully embracing the absurdity of the situation. And so, the boy continued munching on the apple seeds, believing he was gaining wisdom beyond measure. As the days passed, he couldn't help but feel a newfound sense of brilliance with each seed he swallowed. His excitement knew no bounds, and he decided to share this newfound "intelligence" with the world. He set up a pop-up shop on the street corner, proudly displaying a sign that read, "The Brilliant Apple Seed Emporium: Unlock Your Inner Genius!"

Passersby couldn't resist the allure of the quirky display, and soon, a crowd gathered around the young man's stand. He began his pitch, "Step right up, folks! Eat one of these magical seeds, and you'll solve math problems in your sleep! Eat two, and you'll outsmart your annoying little sibling! Eat three, and you'll outwit the most cunning of cats!"

People couldn't help but laugh at his antics, but they were intrigued nonetheless. The news of the "Brilliant Apple Seed Emporium" spread like wildfire, attracting customers from all over the city. With the sudden influx of customers, the boy enlisted the help of his friends to keep up with the demand. They donned silly apple-themed hats and aprons, adding to the hilarity of the situation. The local apple farmers couldn't believe their luck either. They happily joined forces with the young man, providing him with an endless supply of apples and seeds. They, too, were caught up in the contagious laughter and excitement of it all.

As the young man's empire expanded, he decided to host an "Apple Seed Olympics." The event featured quirky competitions like apple seed spitting, apple peeling races, and a hilarious "apple bobbing with hands tied" challenge. People traveled from neighboring towns to witness the spectacle, laughing and cheering as contestants tried their best to showcase their newfound "intelligence" through these comical contests.

But amidst all the laughter, the young man had a compassionate side too. He decided to use a portion of the proceeds to support educational initiatives for underprivileged children. He believed that laughter and intelligence should be accessible to all. And so, the legend of the young man who turned a truck of apples into a laughter-filled sensation continued to grow. People laughed, they ate apple seeds, and they marveled at the magic of it all. Little did they know that the true magic was the joy, camaraderie, and kindness that this quirky adventure brought to their lives. And they all lived, laughing and "intelligent" ever after.

CHAPTER 41 Three astronauts

In the vast expanse of the cosmos, a new agency named "SpaceEarthSky" emerged, revolutionizing space travel for the biggest businesses and making astronauts' journeys more comfortable than ever before. With cutting-edge technologies and a touch of magic, "SpaceEarthSky" aimed to turn space exploration into an enchanting experience.

As the agency prepared for its inaugural space flight, three extraordinary astronauts - Mike, Thomas, and Robin - were chosen for a historic mission. Each of them would embark on a separate spaceship to study different regions of the universe in search of other forms of life.

Mike, the charismatic womanizer of the group, had a unique request for his interstellar journey. He wanted companionship, so he decided to bring along ten beautiful and intelligent women as his crewmates. His rationale was that with such delightful company, the long years in space would feel less lonely and more enjoyable.

Thomas, a self-proclaimed food lover, had his eyes set on an exquisite culinary experience throughout the mission. In the grand spaceship, a luxurious room was reserved, filled to the brim with top-quality food items handpicked by Thomas himself. From tantalizing delicacies to gourmet treats, Thomas was determined to indulge in a gastronomic adventure as he traversed the cosmos.

Lastly, there was Robin, a devoted smoker who simply couldn't break free from his addiction to cigarettes. Despite numerous attempts to quit, he remained a lost cause when it came to kicking the habit. In his spaceship, the cargo hold was stocked with an abundance of cigars and cigarettes, ensuring that Robin had a ready supply to help him relax amidst the challenges of space travel.

As the countdown reached zero, the three spaceships launched into the great unknown, leaving Earth behind for their ten-year expedition. Each astronaut ventured on their distinct mission, armed with the things that brought them joy and comfort.

The years rolled on, and the anticipation grew among the team back on Earth as they eagerly awaited the triumphant return of their intrepid explorers. After what seemed like an eternity, the first spaceship approached, and the hatch opened to reveal Mike standing tall with an entourage of children running around him, accompanied by several women, some of whom were visibly pregnant. With a beaming smile, Mike declared, "Ah, it was a truly successful mission indeed!"

Shortly after, the second spaceship returned, and the tailgate opened to unveil Thomas, whose appearance had significantly changed during the journey. He looked exceedingly happy but noticeably plumper than when he had departed. He explained with enthusiasm, "What an extraordinary journey! The food was out of this world!"

Lastly, the third spaceship descended back to Earth, and the hatch flung open, but the astronaut who emerged was not the calm and composed Robin they knew. Instead, he appeared agitated and irritable, almost like a wild beast. The team greeted him cautiously, asking about his mission, and to everyone's surprise, Robin exclaimed, "WHERE DID YOU PUT THE LIGHTER?!?!?!"

It turned out that amidst the vastness of space and the mesmerizing discoveries they made, Robin's main concern had been finding his lighter. His addiction had not diminished, and the years of space travel hadn't changed his determination to smoke.

Despite the different experiences and priorities, Mike, Thomas, and Robin had achieved something incredible during their ten-year odyssey. They had each found moments of joy, wonder, and challenge in the great beyond, and their adventures would forever be etched in the annals of space exploration history.

The "SpaceEarthSky" agency celebrated its successful mission, and as the astronauts' stories were shared with the world, people marveled at the possibilities of space travel and the diverse personalities of those who ventured to the stars. The mission had not only expanded humanity's knowledge of the universe but had also taught valuable lessons about the resilience and adaptability of the human spirit in the face of the unknown. And so, with their epic journey completed, Mike, Thomas, and Robin entered the pantheon of space pioneers, inspiring future generations to dream of reaching even greater heights among the stars.

CHAPTER 42 Lucy and her Best Friend Milo

Once upon a time, there was a little girl named Lucy, whose world revolved around the warmth of her family and the unconditional love of her furry best friend, Milo. While her two older brothers lived in different cities with their families, Lucy cherished the special bond she shared with her parents, Stan and Lauren, in the cozy family home.

From a young age, Lucy displayed introverted tendencies, preferring the comfort of her home over bustling social gatherings. She found solace in the company of her loyal companion, Milo, a medium-sized golden retriever with a heart of gold. Milo seemed to understand Lucy like no one else, offering quiet companionship during her moments of introspection and unleashing boundless energy for their adventures in the nearby park.

Lucy's favorite part of each day was returning home from school to find Milo waiting eagerly at the door, his wagging tail and twinkling eyes expressing the joy of their reunion. The two of them spent countless hours together, playing fetch in the park or simply lying side by side, savoring the serenity of each other's presence.

Milo's endearing fear of squirrels always brought laughter to Lucy's heart. Watching her otherwise brave and gentle dog flee from the tiny, non-threatening creatures never failed to amuse her. It was as if Milo believed the squirrels possessed some mystical power that rendered them dangerous foes. One bright and warm day in July, Stan surprised Lucy by taking her and Milo on a delightful adventure to a park renowned for its diverse fruit trees.

Their mission for the day was to find the tastiest and juiciest blueberries. The trio set off on their quest, exploring the park's verdant trails and relishing the beauty of nature.

After what seemed like an endless search, they stumbled upon a hidden treasure—a magnificent, flourishing blueberry tree. Lucy's eyes widened with excitement as she picked the ripest, plumpest blueberries with glee. Her heart swelled with gratitude for the special moments shared with her dad and her ever-faithful companion, Milo. Back home, Lucy proudly presented the sweet bounty to her mom, Lauren, who couldn't help but smile at the love and thoughtfulness that filled her daughter's heart. The memory of that summer day lingered in their hearts, forever etched in the tapestry of cherished family moments.

As Lucy matured, she embarked on new adventures. College took her to a different city, and her time with Milo became more limited. Despite the distance, their bond remained unbreakable. Holidays and vacations were always eagerly awaited by both Lucy and Milo, as they cherished every moment they had together. One fateful day, Lucy's life took an unexpected turn when she met a wonderful guy whom she eventually married. Their journey led them to Europe, far from the familiar comforts of home. Although Milo continued to reside with Stan and Lauren, Lucy's heart held a special place for her dear canine companion.

As the years passed, Milo gracefully embraced old age. His once-vibrant energy may have diminished, but his love for Stan and Lauren remained as steadfast as ever. At the ripe age of 12 years and 6 months, Milo's spirit peacefully departed, leaving behind a legacy of love and memories that would forever warm the hearts of those who knew him. To this day, Lucy fondly remembers her time with Milo. When she encounters fruit trees or sees blueberries at the supermarket, a bittersweet smile dances on her lips as she reminisces about her beloved companion. Though Milo may no longer be physically present, his enduring presence lingers in the depths of Lucy's heart, reminding her that the bonds of love are timeless and can span continents and lifetimes. The memories they created together continue to shape Lucy's life, teaching her the true meaning of loyalty, love, and the beauty of simple moments shared with those we hold dear.

As Lucy and her husband strolled through the streets of Europe, she would often find herself sharing stories of Milo, his endearing quirks, and the unconditional love he showered upon her. Her husband listened with rapt attention, captivated by the tale of this special friendship that had left an indelible mark on Lucy's heart. They decided to adopt a rescue dog, inspired by the love Lucy had shared with Milo. Though no dog could ever replace her beloved friend, the new addition to their family brought its own unique charm and joy. Lucy couldn't help but notice the subtle resemblances between their new furry companion and Milo, as if fate had brought them together to continue the legacy of love and devotion. Years passed, and Lucy's life in Europe flourished. She built a fulfilling career, made new friends, and created countless beautiful memories with her husband and their furry family member. Yet, amidst the joy of new adventures, she never forgot the little girl who once roamed the park with a faithful golden retriever by her side. Every time she saw a blueberry or a fruit tree, Lucy couldn't help but be transported back to those carefree days. She treasured the lessons Milo had taught her—about love, loyalty, and the beauty of embracing life's simple pleasures.

Lucy's heart held a special place for Milo, the sweetest of all golden retrievers, who had touched her life in a way that no one else ever could. And so, the tale of Lucy and her cherished friend, Milo, lived on, a timeless testament to the enduring magic of love and the profound impact that our animal companions can have on our lives.

CHAPTER 43 What a beautiful trip!

Mia is now an old lady, and she lives in a nursing home. One day she is talking to her friend Annabelle about her childhood and the two of them start talking about stories they had as kids.

Mia tells her:" When I was 8 or 9 years old, I had the best family trip of my life…" and she smiles from ear to ear and then she continued " It was me, my sister Bella, and my parents. We travelled a few hours by car, and I still remember packing the car and bringing with me my favourite toys… I wonder where I put them, I might have them somewhere…anyway, we got there very early in the morning as my dad wanted to travel before sunrise to then let us enjoy the beach for longer. We packed up the car with all our beach gear and set off early in the morning. As soon as my dad parked the car, I started running towards the coast with my sister. We loved the sea and I remember clearly the waves crashing against the beach, the sound of birds chirping, and the smell of the water of the sea."

Annabelle "Oh, that sounds beautiful. I remember I used to love running on the beach and feeling the warm sand on my feet" She paused for a second and then she added "Good old times…how did you normally spend your days? I used to hate when my brothers pranked me but now that I think about it, I kind of miss those times…" she added, sounding melancholic.

"Me and my sister used to love building sandcastles. We used to spend hours trying to make the best sandcastle we could. It was as high as us, the whole beach would stare at it and take pictures" she added, proud of herself. We also loved collecting seashells… one of the best parts of the day was the late afternoon just before dinner when my mom would give us a lemonade. I remember sipping it on the beach with my sister while looking at the sunset. It was truly beautiful…"

"The most amazing moment was after dinner… we used to be together, and my dad would light the fire and play the guitar. We used to tell each other stories, talk about everything…it was special. I felt so joyful and stressed free…good old time. Spending time with my family as a kid always made me feel special and loved" and then she added "Those were truly unforgettable memories that I will remember till my last day".

CHAPTER 44 Appreciate the Nature

Alessandro's eyes sparkled with excitement as he listened to his grandma's captivating tale of her visit to the Grand Canyon. The whole room was filled with eager anticipation as Carla continued to share her cherished memories.

She began describing their journey across America, how they covered vast distances by car, exploring charming villages and vibrant cities. They had experienced a rich tapestry of cultures, savoring different cuisines, and meeting warm-hearted people along the way. The trip had left an indelible mark on Carla's heart, but it was the day they set their eyes on the Grand Canyon that truly left her in awe.

"We arrived at the Grand Canyon just as the sun was rising," Carla narrated, her voice tinged with nostalgia. "The colors that painted the sky were breathtaking – a tapestry of pinks, oranges, and purples blending into one another. It was like witnessing a masterpiece being created before our very eyes."

She vividly recounted the moment she first laid eyes on the vast expanse of the Grand Canyon, stretching out majestically as far as the eye could see. "I felt so small in comparison to the grandeur of nature around me. The immensity of the canyon, the layers of rock, and the deep crevices left me in a state of wonderment. It's one thing to see pictures of it, but being there in person is an entirely different experience."

Carla's storytelling transported everyone to the edge of the canyon, where they imagined themselves taking in the awe-inspiring vistas. As they munched on their lasagna and sipped their wine, the family was spellbound by her words. The sandwiches that her mom had prepared became a focal point of the story, representing not just a meal but a symbol of togetherness and shared experiences. As they imagined the scene, they could almost taste the sandwiches themselves and feel the joyous atmosphere of that moment.

"I remember sitting with my family, munching on those delicious sandwiches while gazing out at the mesmerizing landscape," Carla continued. "It felt like we were connected to something far greater than ourselves. The Grand Canyon has a way of making you feel both humbled and privileged to witness such natural beauty."

Carla's tale continued with stories of playful squirrels darting around, the sound of birds singing in the distance, and the cool breeze that carried the scent of pine. "It was a moment of serenity and appreciation for the wonders of our planet. When you stand at the edge of the canyon, you realize how small and fleeting our existence is in comparison to the enduring magnificence of nature."

Her words resonated deeply with Alessandro, and he could hardly wait for his own journey to the Grand Canyon. He wondered what emotions would wash over him when he finally stood at the rim, witnessing its grandeur firsthand. The family was in rapt attention as Carla wrapped up her narrative. "It was a transformative experience, one that stays with you for a lifetime," she concluded with a smile. "I hope you all get to see it someday and feel the same sense of awe and wonder. It truly is a treasure of our planet."

As the conversation shifted to other topics, Alessandro found himself gazing out the window, lost in thoughts of the upcoming adventure. He knew that when he finally set foot on that hallowed ground, he would carry with him the legacy of his grandma's story and appreciate the Grand Canyon with a heart full of gratitude and reverence for the marvels of nature.

The family lunch continued, filled with laughter, joy, and excitement for the journey that awaited Alessandro. And in the days leading up to his departure, he found himself eagerly counting down the moments until he, too, would be mesmerized by the splendor of the Grand Canyon and create his own cherished memories to share with generations to come.

CHAPTER 45 The Beauty of the Snow

Tom and Max continued reminiscing about their past adventures and experiences, sipping on hot cups of coffee in a cozy café. Tom went on, "You know, Max, Switzerland is like a winter wonderland. The landscapes are breathtaking, and the air feels so crisp and pure. I remember waking up early every morning, excited to hit the ski slopes. My parents would bundle us up in layers of warm clothing, and off we went, like little snow explorers."

Max chuckled, "I can imagine you as a little snow explorer, Tom! I hope my kids will be just as thrilled about the snow as you were. I'm sure they'll love it, though; kids usually do."

"Definitely! And even if they don't take to skiing right away, there are plenty of other fun activities they can enjoy," Tom assured him. "In the afternoons, after skiing, my brother and I would take naps to recharge, and then we'd head out for some playful snowball fights and building snowmen. Those moments were pure joy."

Max smiled, "Snowball fights and snowmen sound like a lot of fun! I can't wait to see my kids' faces light up when they experience snow for the first time. It's going to be magical."

"It truly is," Tom agreed. "And the evenings were just as enchanting. The village we stayed in had a cozy, fairytale-like charm. We would take leisurely walks with our parents, exploring hidden nooks and crannies. My dad would call them 'adventures,' and it made us feel like we were on some grand quest. We'd meet friendly locals, share stories, and even try traditional Swiss delicacies."

Max's eyes sparkled with excitement, "That sounds like the perfect family adventure! I can't wait to create those special memories with my own family."

As they sipped their coffee, Tom's nostalgia grew even stronger. "You know, Max, what amazed me the most was the sense of timelessness. In Switzerland, time seemed to slow down, and all the worries and stresses of everyday life melted away. It felt like we were living in a snow globe, wrapped in a serene bubble of happiness and tranquility."

"That sounds like a dream come true," Max said wistfully. "In our fast-paced lives, it's rare to find such moments of pure peace and contentment."

"It truly was," Tom said, a dreamy smile forming on his face. "And the memories of that trip have stayed with me all these years. Switzerland has a way of capturing your heart and leaving a lasting impression."

As the two friends continued chatting, they couldn't help but get lost in the magic of their shared memories. Tom's stories ignited a newfound excitement in Max as he eagerly anticipated his upcoming family trip to Switzerland. They made plans to exchange photos and stories when Max returned, promising to relive the joys of their friendship through these cherished memories. In that cozy café, surrounded by the buzz of life outside, Tom and Max found solace in their nostalgic conversation. They realized that no matter how much time had passed since they last met, their friendship remained as strong as ever, bonded by the shared adventures of their past and the anticipation of creating new memories in the future. And so, they looked forward to the day when Max's family would embark on their Swiss journey, weaving their own tapestry of happiness and creating memories to last a lifetime.

CHAPTER 46 New experiences

"Two weeks ago, we went to Chile with Becky and the kids," said Roger to his co-worker Jack.

"Oh really, I have never been there. How is it?"

Roger replied" It was different than what I thought it would be. I thought it was going to be more chaotic and busier than it was. All the people that I know that have been there have told me that it can get very loud during the day and night and the streets are packed with people, especially in the evening".

"That would be my worst nightmare," Jack replied.

"I know. I did not think my kids would like it, but Becky needed to be there for work and everything for us was paid for, so we went anyway."

"Did the kids like it?"

"They loved it! I was a bit nervous at first because it was such an unfamiliar place, and I did not know my way around there. I wanted them to have a great experience and got a bit stressed because I did not know if I could do it… and then he added "I did not much about the local culture, but while Becky was busy for work me and the kids walked around for the city, and it felt like such a friendly and warm place. People were extremely friendly with us and with my kids. We went to a restaurant, and they gave a cake for free to my kids… here it never happened!"

"WOW!" Jack exclaimed, "I am moving there!"

"There are lots of museums and a few important landmarks that we visited, and it was nice. Overall, it was nice visiting another country with a completely different culture and language".

"Did your wife get to see the city too or she was working the whole time?"

"She was busy most of the day, but we would walk together in the evening along the coast and every single day there was like a big party there. I do not know if that happens all year round, but when we went it felt like there was a festival every evening".

"I have kids too; I will add Chile to my bucket list" Jack replied.

"Absolutely! My kids are 7 and 12. It was nice to see how much they grew after visiting a foreign country. I feel like it opened their minds. They even made friends with some kids there. They have their Instagram, and it is nice to know that my kids already have friends from people somewhere else in the world… I don't even know anyone outside my city" and started laughing.

"Especially as kids they need to step out of their comfort zone and see new places. I am sure that will benefit them a lot in the future. That sounds like such a wonderful holiday… and on top of that, you did not even spend much! Wow! I am going!" Jack said to his friend.

CHAPTER 47 A Loved Volleyball Coach

Josephine had lived a life full of passion, dedication, and love for the sport she held so dear. As a former professional volleyball player, she had experienced the thrill of victory, the agony of defeat, and the camaraderie of being part of a team. Even in her seventies, her heart still beat with the rhythm of the game, and she couldn't imagine a life without volleyball.

After retiring from her professional career, Josephine knew she couldn't leave the sport behind. Coaching became her new calling, her way of passing on her knowledge and love for volleyball to the younger generation. She dedicated herself wholeheartedly to teaching the sport to young kids, instilling in them not just the skills to excel on the court, but also the values of teamwork, perseverance, and sportsmanship. For years, Josephine's coaching journey had been a rewarding one. Seeing the young athletes grow, improve, and find joy in the sport brought immeasurable happiness to her soul. Her love for children made every day spent with her young athletes feel like a gift. As she stood on the sidelines, observing their progress and witnessing their smiles, she knew that she had found her purpose in life. But as the January chill settled in, Josephine found herself facing an unexpected challenge. Health issues began to take a toll on her body, leaving her fatigued and in need of rest. It was a difficult decision to make, but she knew she had to take a break from coaching to focus on her well-being. The news came as a surprise to her young athletes, who had grown to adore their coach and saw her as a guiding light.

The last game of the season in August marked the end of an era. It was an emotional day as Josephine bid farewell to her team, her heart heavy with gratitude and pride. Little did she know that her young athletes had something special planned for her, a surprise that would forever remain etched in her heart. As the final whistle blew, the team gathered on the court, each player holding a single rose. They formed a line, creating a colorful bouquet of gratitude and love. With tears in their eyes and hearts full of appreciation, they presented the massive set of roses to their beloved coach. Josephine's eyes widened with astonishment and joy as she held the bouquet in her hands.

"Thank you, Coach Josephine, for everything you've done for us," one of the players said, her voice trembling with emotion.

"You believed in us even when we didn't believe in ourselves," another player added, tears streaming down her cheeks.

The players took turns expressing their gratitude, sharing how Josephine's guidance and encouragement had transformed their lives on and off the court. Josephine felt a swell of emotions in her chest, her heart overflowing with love and pride for her team. The gymnasium echoed with cheers and applause as the players, parents, and coaches joined in celebrating Josephine's legacy. It was a moment of pure joy and camaraderie, a testament to the impact Josephine had on those around her.

After the heartfelt tribute, the team decided to turn the occasion into a proper celebration. They set up a makeshift party area in the gym, complete with tables adorned with cheerful decorations, delicious food, and lively music. The gymnasium, once filled with the echoes of sportsmanship, was now alive with laughter, conversations, and the spirit of friendship.

Summer had embraced the evening, and the golden sunlight poured through the windows, casting a warm glow on the partygoers. Josephine found herself surrounded by the young athletes she had mentored, their parents, fellow coaches, and friends. The atmosphere was filled with love, appreciation, and a shared passion for the sport that had brought them all together. As the night progressed, stories were shared, memories were made, and the bond between the team members grew even stronger. They danced, laughed, and reminisced about the victories and challenges they had faced together.

For Josephine, this party was a treasure beyond measure. It was a testament to the profound impact she had on the lives of these young athletes. It was a reminder of the joy and fulfillment she had found in coaching, the same joy that had fueled her passion for volleyball since she was a young girl. Months passed, and Josephine's heart held onto the memory of that special day. Whenever she saw roses, whether in a florist shop or on the streets, her heart would flutter with joy and gratitude. Those flowers became a symbol of the love, appreciation, and bond she had shared with her team.

As she continued her journey of recovery, the memory of that heartfelt tribute served as a source of strength and motivation. The love and support of her young athletes, parents, and fellow coaches had ignited a fire within her soul, urging her to overcome her health challenges and return to the court. During her break from coaching, Josephine took the time to reflect on her coaching philosophy and techniques. She poured herself into books, attending coaching seminars, and researching the latest trends in the sport. Her passion for learning and improving herself had not waned over the years, and she was determined to come back stronger than ever.

Spring arrived with a sense of renewal, and Josephine's health showed signs of improvement. Her doctor was pleased with her progress and gave her the green light to ease back into coaching. The news filled Josephine's heart with hope and excitement. She couldn't wait to be back on the court, sharing her love for volleyball with her young athletes once more. When the new season began, Josephine returned to the gymnasium with a renewed sense of purpose and determination. Her young athletes welcomed her back with open arms and radiant smiles. It was as if a missing piece had been restored, completing the puzzle of their volleyball journey.

Josephine knew that she had been given a second chance to make a difference in the lives of her young athletes. With each practice, she brought her trademark passion, patience, and expertise, encouraging her players to reach new heights and embrace the joy of the game. As the summer sun bathed the gymnasium in its warm glow, Josephine looked around at her young athletes, their eyes shining with determination. The memories of that special party in August, the roses, and the heartfelt expressions of gratitude flooded her mind.

Every day, Josephine continued to pass on the legacy of love and dedication that had defined her own journey as a volleyball player and coach. The gymnasium echoed with the sound of volleyballs being spiked, the laughter of young athletes, and the unwavering commitment of a coach who had given her heart and soul to the sport she cherished. And so, the story of Josephine, the volleyball coach who found joy in mentoring young athletes, continued to unfold. Her journey became a beacon of inspiration, reminding all who crossed her path of the profound impact that love, dedication, and a shared passion for the game could have on one's life.

As she walked through the park on a bright summer day, Josephine couldn't help but smile as she spotted a young couple, the guy giving a bouquet of roses to his girlfriend. The sight filled her heart with warmth, and she felt an overwhelming sense of gratitude for the love and appreciation she had received from her young athletes.Each time she saw roses, Josephine was transported back to that magical evening in August, a memory she treasured for the rest of her life. It was a reminder that love, in all its forms, had the power to leave an indelible mark on the human heart.

In her seventies, Josephine had found her life's purpose, not just in the sport of volleyball, but in the hearts of the young athletes she mentored. The roses served as a constant reminder of the love, gratitude, and joy that had blossomed in the gymnasium that summer evening, forever etched in the tapestry of her coaching legacy. And so, as the seasons continued to change, Josephine's love for volleyball and her young athletes remained as timeless and enduring as the beauty of a blooming rose.

CHAPTER 48 Miami: A Special Place

Miami. 12th August. 8.23 pm.

Lars and Svela are a Swedish couple. They plan to go on holiday in Miami this year and finally, the time has come.

Lars has been planning on how to propose for a while now. A few days before their flight he was talking to his sister talking through what the plan was and asked for advice. After he finished explaining to her what the plan was she said "OMG, this seems like a movie! She is going to love it".

So, that evening the couple was walking along the beach. He asked them to take a few pictures of him so that he could show his parents how beautiful the view is. After taking a few pictures with the sun in the background that began to disappear, making the sky look like a mix of orange and red., an outstanding view: he asked her to join him. He went to set the camera telling his soon-to-be fiancée that he was going to set the 10-second timer after pressing the button, while the truth is that he just started a video. So, he rushed next to his wife, and they posed to take a very romantic picture. After that, they left the camera where it was just a few meters from them, and they stared at the horizon in a very romantic setting.

Svela always loved walking barefoot on the sand and staring at the sunset. Lars knew this about her and wanted her to receive the proposal in this scenario. After a while, they were about to come back to the hotel where they would have prepared before going to the restaurant.

Lars pointed to a few birds flying in the sky and said, "That is so beautiful, it feels so peaceful here", Svela smiled and nodded.

Then he pointed somewhere else so that Svela could turn, and he could bend his knee and proposed and said "Look at that! Wow!". Svela turned, and asked, "Where? I cannot see anything?". No reply. So, she turned and found Lars bending on one knee while holding a ring.

He looked into her eyes; they were both feeling very emotional. He prepared a whole speech, but it felt like the words would not come out. He eventually said, "Svela, will you marry me?" Svela was speechless too, her hands covering half of her face and the joy radiating from her eyes. She was over the moon.

Before putting the ring on her finger, he told her how much he loved her and was able to make the speech she prepared for so long, talking about their relationship and how much he was eager to spend the rest of his life with her.

She was crying, she nodded, said " I love you" and let Lars put the ring on her finger.

They hugged straight after, he grabbed her waist, and she grabbed hir back. They kissed, looked each other in the eyes, and started laughing.

They walked back towards the hotel feeling super happy. They could not believe what was happening. It felt like a dream.

Since then, every time they hear "Miami " they would think of that moment, and they knew that was one of the most important and special moments of their life.

CHAPTER 49 An Unusual Situation

Mario is a dentist and like every Sunday he is going to have lunch with his family.

It is a tradition that they have had since Mario and his younger brother Ninno moved out of the house. Mario and his wife and kids show up at his parents' house on time. However, Ninno showed up late with his fiance.

The Sunday lunch together is the moment when they catch up and enjoy time with their loved ones.

Mario loves telling them stories and at some point, he tells his family about this new patient. A young man, very friendly and nice, but after a few appointments Mario noticed that he was a bit worried for the young lad as he would forget the sessions before.

"What do you mean by "he forgets the sessions"? asked his dad.

"It seems like he does not remember what I told him during the session before. It seems like he does not even remember my name. It seems like it is always session one" Mario said and then added "What do you think I should do?" looking at his family and asking for a piece of genuine advice.

"For starters, I would ask him to pay you before the sessions...," said his brother.

Everyone laughed.

CHAPTER 50 Ice Cream and Sweets

Sarah and Tom are a very religious couple. They go to church every Sunday and they try to help other people in any way they can. This is the same belief that their son learned; their motto is "Sharing is caring".

Sarah and their sons leave the house to go buy groceries. When they walked out of the shop while the mom was busy with putting the bags in the car, her kid saw a homeless person on the other side of the road and asked her mom.

"Mom, can I please have $5?"

"What for?" replies the mom.

"There is a homeless person on the other side of the road."

"Where can I see him?"

"Over their mom," said the kid while pointing at the homeless and added "The one that is screaming "I want ice cream! I want sweets!"

CHAPTER 51 Dogs Are Not Allowed in the Shop

Milan. 16th August. 9.45 am.

A man in his 40s walks into a bar with his dog, Molly, and heads to the counter to order his usual breakfast: cappuccino and almond croissant. Before he even sits down to order the barista looks at him and while he is making coffee for another customer says: "Excuse me, sir, dogs are not allowed to enter this establishment. I'm sorry, but those are the rules."

The man replies:" This is my guide dog, I am blind."

"Oh, I see, I'm so sorry," says the bartender, "I'm mortified, I didn't realize that. It's okay then, don't worry, and sorry again."

The two begin to talk about animals, and the barista explains that he loves dogs, but unfortunately in his experience, he has seen quite a few dogs come into the bar and do damage, so he decided to prevent dogs from being allowed in.

A few minutes later, shortly after the first gentleman left the shop, another man entered the bar with a poodle.

The gentleman seems a little drunk. He keeps bumping into tables and other people. The bartender, who is also the owner of the bar, tells the new customer that dogs are not allowed.

No answer.

So, he repeats: "Excuse me, sir, dogs are not allowed."

And the dog's owner replies: "It's a guide dog! I'm blind."

The bartender replies: "I don't think so, poodles are not dogs for blind people!"

The man pauses for a moment and then replies, "What?!? They gave me a poodle?! That is why I bump into everything everywhere... I got scammed."

CHAPTER 52 Hunting

Elizabeth is the youngest sister of three. She has just turned 19 and on her birthday, she met a boy, Valentin and the two started dating.

His siblings, Leon and Bea cannot wait to meet him. Elizabeth talks about her boyfriend all the time. So, one day they all plan to meet up at their parents' house. They often have family meetings where they enjoy each other's company. This time, Valentin will be also invited.

As he shows up there, he has been greeted very nicely by Elizabeth's family and they seem to get on quite well. Soon after he starts talking with Leon and Robert, Elizabeth's father, about football and sports in general.

Valentin is a very friendly guy with a good sense of humor, and it is not hard for him to be liked by other people.

He starts telling Leon that he enjoys hunting with his friends and that recently he hunted the biggest bear in the world.

He said that he had gone to a small village in the north of Sweden where there are more bears than people. He was there with his friend, and they noticed a small cave. They went in, but there was a little bear. At a distance of a few meters, they noticed a slightly larger cave, of medium size and there was a medium bear. They notice a much larger cave in the distance, happy to have finally found the place they have been waiting for…

Leon interrupts him: "And you saw the massive bear?"

"No, there was a library inside."

CHAPTER 53 Graduation Day

Isabella's eyes sparkled with nostalgia as she continued to share the story of her graduation day with her friend Ava at the nursing home. The memories flooded back, transporting her to that momentous day in her youth.

"After the dinner, my friends and I decided to go for a walk in the city. The streets were alive with celebration and joy. It felt like the whole world was rejoicing with us. We laughed, we danced, and we made promises to stay in touch and support each other as we ventured into the next chapter of our lives."

Ava smiled warmly, hanging onto Isabella's every word. "It sounds like a dream come true, Isabella. Your graduation day was truly magical."

"It was," Isabella agreed. "But you know, the magic didn't end there. In the days that followed, I received so many congratulatory messages and gifts from friends and family. I felt overwhelmed by the love and support I had around me. It was like the universe was telling me that my hard work was recognized and appreciated."

Ava leaned in, intrigued by Isabella's story. "And what did you do next? Where did life take you after such a momentous day?"

Isabella's smile widened as she recalled the journey that followed. "After graduation, I went to college to pursue my passion for literature. It was a whole new chapter in my life, filled with learning, growth, and new experiences. I met amazing people, made lifelong friends, and discovered my true calling as a writer."

"Wow, you are truly inspiring, Isabella," Ava remarked. "Your determination and hard work have taken you far."

"I believe that day, my graduation day, was the turning point for me," Isabella said thoughtfully. "It was the day I realized that with dedication and perseverance, I could achieve anything I set my mind to. My parents' pride and happiness in my accomplishments gave me the confidence to pursue my dreams fearlessly."

As they chatted, other residents of the nursing home joined them, drawn by the captivating conversation. Isabella's story had touched their hearts, and they wanted to hear more about her remarkable journey. With a smile, Isabella obliged, recounting the adventures she had in her writing career. She spoke of the joy of seeing her words come to life in print, of the satisfaction of touching hearts and minds with her stories, and of the countless lives she had touched through her work. As the evening sun painted the room with warm hues, Isabella's storytelling filled the space with a sense of wonder and hope. Her tale of resilience, love, and determination resonated deeply with everyone present. It reminded them all that no matter their age or circumstances, they could still dream, achieve, and make a difference.

The nursing home became a hub of encouragement and support, with residents sharing their own stories of triumph and accomplishment. Each person had a unique journey to share, and they discovered that they were not alone in their struggles and triumphs. In the weeks that followed, Isabella and Ava became close friends, cherishing each other's company and learning from each other's experiences. They laughed, they cried, and they encouraged one another to keep chasing their dreams, no matter how big or small.

The nursing home blossomed into a community of camaraderie and inspiration, with residents supporting each other in their pursuits and celebrating each other's milestones. Isabella's graduation day story became a symbol of hope and possibility, a reminder that life's most beautiful moments could happen at any age. As Isabella's words spread, their impact reached beyond the nursing home's walls. Families and friends of the residents were moved by the stories of resilience and determination, and they started visiting more often, sharing their own stories of love and support. The power of storytelling brought together people from all walks of life, reminding them that every day held the potential for magic and miracles. Isabella's graduation day remained a cherished memory, not only for her but for everyone who had the privilege of hearing her tale. And so, the legacy of that special day lived on, weaving a tapestry of joy, love, and inspiration in the hearts of those who shared in Isabella's story. As the sun set on another beautiful day, Isabella and her friends at the nursing home looked forward to creating new memories, knowing that each day was a gift filled with endless possibilities.

CHAPTER 54 Eternal Love

Once upon a time in a small village near Texas, there was Benjamin, an old man that lived most of his life in a modest house built a few meters from a cemetery. The village where he lives is pretty small and everyone knows each other. Samir is a man in his seventies and is known for being a man of very few words but able to communicate a lot with his eyes.

For anyone that meets him, he seems the kind of man that went through a lot in his life and despite that, he seems to be having a very peaceful energy and calm mind.

He spends most of his time in his house. He would leave the house twice a day, once in the morning and once in the afternoon. In the morning, he usually goes to the nearest lake and likes to meditate over there and write his journal while looking at the wonderful view that nature offers.

He enjoys living by himself and the people of the village wonder why such a handsome and smart man never got married.

As years go by, he starts to feel weaker and weaker, and he is rarely seen outside the house. The only times people would see him is when he leaves his house to visit the cemetery. Normally, in the early hours of the morning.

His sister starts to be worried about his condition and so she decides to move back to the village to look after his brother. She moves into a house not far from Benjamin. Sarah would spend her day with his brother and occasionally leave his son, Miro, with his brother just if she had to go shopping in the city a few kilometres away.

One day, while Miro was playing in the living room and his uncle was laying on the couch, Miro noticed a butterfly coming inside the house. It was a beautiful butterfly, full of different bright colours. The butterfly sits on Benjamin's hand for a while and then flies away toward the cemetery.

Miro followed her and saw the butterfly on top of a grave not far from Benjamin's room window. In fact, from his uncle's room, it was possible to see the butterfly.

He went back to the house and kept playing, while his uncle seemed to sleep peacefully.

A few minutes later, Sarah came back home and realized that his beloved brother passed away in his sleep. She knew he did not have long left to live and expected it to happen, even though she felt extremely sad she tried to be strong for Miro. Miro told her about the beautiful butterfly and Sarah said:

"Son, you have to know that your uncle 50 years ago was going to get married to a beautiful and sweet girl, Hannah, but she passed away a few days before the wedding. She was buried in that grave where you saw the butterfly go. Your uncle built this house to be close to her and promised to himself that he would never marry another girl and that he would live his life at the best he could despite the heart-breaking news because that is what Hannah would have wanted."

Miro said, "Oh, so now Uncle Benjamin is with his girlfriend, isn't he?"

"Yes, he is," replied Sarah, while smiling at his son."

An eternal love.

CHAPTER 55 "What is politics?"

A child is watching TV, turns, and asks his father: "Dad what is politics?"

"Why? Is it something you have to know for school?" replied the father wondering why his 7 years old kid wants to know about it.

"No, I heard it on TV just now".

The father thinks about it and then says: "I'll explain it to you with an example" and then said, " Imagine this: I work and bring home the money, so I am the capitalist: your mother who administers it, is the government; the cleaning woman is the working class; you who now have some say are the people; your sister who has just been born is the future."

The child says," I do not understand."

"You will soon, trust me," says the father.

The child goes to sleep, but in the middle of the night, he wakes up because his sister starts crying. The child gets up from his bed and wants to tell his father that his sister is crying but cannot find him. His mother won't wake up. He goes to the room in the basement where the cleaning lady lives, and the door is locked, and he could hear his father's voice there too. So, he comes back to bed while his sister is still screaming and crying.

While lying on the bed he reflects on his father's words and thinks to himself: "I think I know what politics is now: the capitalists screw the working class, the government sleeps, the people are ignored, and the future is terrible"

CHAPTER 56 "You would better get another job"

Lukasz is a young man who has always been interested in politics. His grandad was a famous politician who spent his life in politics until the last day of his life. Since he was a teenager, Lukasz read articles and books about anything related to politics, with the goal of becoming a politician and improving the condition of his country.

Finally, when Lukasz is old enough, he joins the party to enter politics. On his first day, the party secretary, to test him, pretends to lose £100. This is a test that the party secretary has often done to new people.

The young man, unaware, finds it and promptly returns it to him. He tells him, "Excuse me, you dropped this."

The politician immediately says to him, "You'd better get another job," and he incredulously says, "Why?" The politician replies, "Because to be in politics you need someone who will make the money disappear and not find it again."

Lukasz, with a hint of disappointment in his voice, responds firmly, "Respectfully, I must disagree. In politics, our duty is to serve the people, to be honest and transparent. It is not about personal gain or making money disappear. My goal is to work for the betterment of our country and its citizens."

The party secretary raises an eyebrow, taken aback by Lukasz's response. He studies the young man for a moment before nodding thoughtfully.

"Your grandfather was a remarkable politician," the party secretary says, his tone softening. "He was known for his integrity and dedication to the people. I see that you share those traits with him."

Lukasz feels a surge of pride hearing those words. His grandfather had been his greatest inspiration, and being compared to him was an immense honor.

"Thank you," Lukasz replies sincerely. "I hope to live up to his legacy and make him proud."

Over the following weeks and months, Lukasz continues to prove himself within the party. He actively participates in debates, presents well-researched policy proposals, and shows a genuine interest in understanding the needs of the citizens. As Lukasz's reputation grows, he begins to gain the respect and admiration of his fellow party members. Many start to see the value in having a principled and sincere politician among them. With time, Lukasz's hard work and dedication pay off, and he earns the opportunity to run for office. His campaign is centered on transparency, accountability, and a commitment to listening to the voices of the people.

During the election period, Lukasz travels tirelessly across the country, meeting with citizens from all walks of life. He listens to their concerns, hopes, and dreams, and promises to be their voice in the political arena. The election day arrives, and Lukasz stands with a mix of nerves and excitement. He knows that the journey ahead will be challenging, but he is determined to make a positive impact and serve the people with utmost dedication. As the votes are counted, Lukasz's heart pounds with anticipation. And when the results are announced, he can't believe his ears. He has won! The joy and sense of fulfillment that flood his heart are indescribable.

As a newly elected politician, Lukasz remains true to his values. He continues to work tirelessly for the welfare of his country and its people, never losing sight of his initial goal of making a difference. Throughout his political career, Lukasz faces both triumphs and challenges, but he always approaches each situation with integrity and a genuine desire to serve. He gains the respect and trust of the citizens and becomes a beloved figure in the political landscape.

As he looks back on his journey, Lukasz feels a profound sense of gratitude. He knows that he owes his success not only to his determination but also to the teachings and inspiration he received from his grandfather.

In the years that follow, Lukasz's passion for politics and dedication to the people remain unwavering. He becomes a shining example of a politician who defies the norms, proving that honesty and integrity can indeed thrive in the world of politics. Lukasz's story inspires a new generation of aspiring politicians, reminding them that with sincerity, determination, and a genuine love for their country, they too can make a lasting impact on the lives of their fellow citizens.

And so, Lukasz's journey continues, and the legacy of his grandfather lives on through his dedication to serving the people and bringing about positive change in his beloved country. As he walks the path of politics, he knows that he is not only fulfilling his dream but also upholding the values that have been passed down to him by his greatest role model, his beloved grandad.

CHAPTER 57 Karma

Patricia comes home tired after a day at work. Her husband is currently unemployed, and she comes home to find her husband slumped on the couch.

"Jack the gate below won't open," she says to her husband.

The husband, annoyed that his wife will not let him relax, says "I'm not a locksmith."

Patricia sighs disappointed and after a few minutes says:

"Also, the light in the kitchen doesn't work."

The husband replies: "I wish I could fix it, but I am not an electrician."

A few minutes later the wife notices that the bathroom door is rubbing on the floor, and she tells her husband. As usual, he replies that he is not a carpenter and cannot fix it.

The husband realizes that he can't relax when his wife is around so he decides to go to the bar a few yards from her house. He spends a few hours there drinking and having fun with his friends. Once he comes back home, he notices that the gate opens smoothly, the light in the kitchen is working and the bathroom door is not rubbing against the floor anymore.

So, he asks his wife how she was able to fix everything, and she said that her neighbour, after having heard their conversation, offered to help.

Jack replied "WOW! He must have charged us a lot; how much did he ask?"

Patricia replied: "he said you can either make me a cake or give me $500".

"Nice!" said his husband relieved that they paid for all of that with a cake and he asked his wife "And you made him the cake, didn't you?"

"Jack! I am not a baker".

CHAPTER 58 Cheap Uncle

It is a very warm day in Liverpool when in one of the parks in the city two brothers 11, Michael, and 12 years old, Max, are playing football. They are laughing, kicking the ball and they are not aware that while they are doing this, they are building what is going to be remembered as the "Good Old Days".

After hours of playing football, they want to go and play table soccer at the building not far from them.

They love playing table soccer and with the other kids of the city, they always plan little competitions and tournaments that can go on for hours.

While they are walking towards the building Max says "I would love to play but I do not have a single penny in my pocket"

"Me neither" replies Michael and added, "then how do we do it?"

Max went quiet thinking of a solution and then said, "Let's go and hope that on the way there we meet my uncle who will give us money to play."

At one point they catch a glimpse of Uncle Thomas.

"Let's go and say hello to him, maybe he'll give us a few pounds to play with," said Max.

"Uncle Thomas is very cheap," said Michael.

"Leave it to me," said Max and then start talking to their uncle: "Hi uncle, how are you? Do you know I dreamed about you last night?".

"Oh Really!? How was the dream?" replied Thomas.

"I dreamed that you gave me 2 pounds to play table soccer" Max replied.

"Really?" said the uncle, sounding surprised by his nephew's dream.

"Yes, uncle, you gave me 2 pounds".

"I understand..." the uncle replied. Then, paused for a moment and added "However little Max don't worry I don't want it back." and walked away, leaving the kids speechless.

CHAPTER 59 100 Walls

There is a prison in Colombia that is known to keep the worst murderers and killers. It is pretty much impossible to escape. It is in the middle of nowhere, there are 100 walls from the jail to the outside world, making it incredibly difficult for anyone to try to escape.

However, after months of planning their escape, two prisoners have a plan to distract the guards and start climbing over the walls.

They are both incredibly fit, so they manage to quickly climb the first few walls at pace.

On the 30th one asks the other "Are you tired?" and the other says "No.

After climbing a few walls, one asks the other " I am starting to feel a bit tired, are you tired?"

The other replies "No, I am not! We are probably halfway. We must finish".

At the 99th they are both exhausted. They can barely walk; they are almost out but the last wall seems like a big challenge. Before trying to climb, one asks the other "Are you tired?" and the other says "Yes, I do not feel my legs anymore, I do not think I can do it."

The other replies "Me too"

"Okay, let's go back then".

They start climbing the 99 walls to go back.

CHAPTER 60 Six Blind Men

A young man by the name of Lukasz used to live in a little village. Lukasz had understood the significance of employment and the value it added to someone's existence since he was a young child. His parents had taught him that a person could achieve great things and find pleasure by working honestly and diligently.

But as he got older, Lukasz started to underestimate the significance of work. The desire to enjoy life without thinking about hard work fascinated him. He was unproductive and spent his days doing nothing.

A knowledgeable village elder noticed the difference in Lukasz one day. Approaching him with a gentle smile, he said, "Young friend, work is like a thread we weave into the fabric of our lives. Your future will be fragile and empty if you don't weave that thread.

Lukasz realized it was time to shift his outlook and value work after hearing the man's words. He decided to pursue a career of growth both personally and professionally.

Lukasz started to put more effort into his work. He was enthusiastic about his duties, did study, and picked up new abilities. He soon started to see the results of his efforts. His output increased, the growth potential appeared, and people began to respect him more.

Lukasz eventually achieved the success he wanted. His personal life, as well as his professional life both, improved. He learned that work was a source of connection with others, fulfillment, and more than just a way to make money.

Lukasz came to understand that having a job was a pleasure as much as a need. He gained the ability to appreciate every facet of his profession and to persevere in the face of difficulties. He inspired others by sharing his experience.

The story's lesson is that work is an essential component of who we are. Self-actualization, satisfaction, and success can all be achieved with a lot of work. Never should we lose sight of how crucial it is to respect our work and give it our all. Because work is the key to achieving our goals and guaranteeing a promising future.

CHAPTER 61 "Honey, you are beautiful"

Mrs. Bentley is an old woman in her eighties.

Since she was in her late twenties, she worried about getting older and every birthday she would tell herself how old she was. She also had low self-esteem and always thought she was not pretty. Her boyfriend at the time told her that she was young and beautiful and there was no reason for her to call herself old. Everyone told her how beautiful she was because she was a beautiful girl. She would thank them, but deep down she would not believe them.

As she grew older, and she got in her fifties she started looking at pictures of herself in her twenties and commenting that she looked beautiful and young. Her husband was happy to hear that and reminded her that he used to tell her that every day, but she would not believe him.

Now, even though she is older, she is still a very good-looking woman, and her husband still tells her every day, but she would reply "No, I am not. Look at me, I am 50. I am not young and not beautiful".

Her husband would tell her "Honey, you are beautiful, and you have many years ahead of you. You never believe you are beautiful. It took you 30 years to see that when you were in your twenties you were gorgeous...I am sure that in a few years, you will see how beautiful you are now"?

She would listen to the sweet words of her husband and think to herself that she was beautiful at the time, but not now.

She is now 82 years old and a widow. One day she is looking after her grandkids at her house. One of her grandkids asks her "Nanny, do you have some pictures of when you were a teenager?". Mrs. Bentley hates pictures and hates showing pictures to anyone, but she cannot say no to her grandkid. So, she goes to her room and takes an album full of pictures.

As they look at the pictures, she comes across a picture of her thirty years before. She looks at it and one of the grandkids says "Wow, you look beautiful in this picture". She smiles, thanks her, and thinks to herself "I was beautiful... how could I not see that? I wish I was that young and that beautiful..."

CHAPTER 62 It is Never too Late

Mr. Hutney is an 85-year-old man.

He started to work after high school and retired just 10 years ago. He needed to start work at an early age because his parents were struggling financially. He had a dream of becoming a writer but could not do anything about it as he did not have time to do it. He did not have an easy childhood, anyone would be feeling sad, but Ted was not like any other kid, he would always have a smile on his face. On Saturday night, he would see his friends going out and having fun while he was working in a restaurant as a waiter in the evening and as a mechanic in the day. Still, he was happy, he seemed to have a special aura about him. Eventually, he made enough money to pay for his education and got a degree. He became an accountant. He would work his 9 to 5 and then come home and spend time with his wife and kids. In his spare time, he writes books trying to improve his skill and make it become its main income. However, he had to stop that soon as his family struggled financially as the cost of living increased and her wife lost her job. Despite that, Mr. Bentley did what he always does. He went to work and never let adversity make him feel sorry for himself. So, he got an evening job at a pub, to provide for his family.

Only in his late seventies, he was able to find some time to do what he always wanted to do: write books. He retired at 75 and from then started working on his books. In 10 years, he wrote over a dozen books, four of which became bestsellers.

Dreams are possible, never let anything stand in your way. Accept the situation, be patient, and never stop dreaming. It is never too late.

CHAPTER 63 Retirement is the Real Beginning

Mrs. Everson is a lady in her sixties, divorced with no kids. She always wanted children in her life, but it never happened. She worked her whole life in a retail shop not far from her house, and she was loved there. Over the years, she met some wonderful people who became like a second family to her. She loved her job; it could be stressful and busy at times, but she handled it very well, and as she always said, "Busy is better. Time flies when it is busy."

One of the main reasons why Mrs. Everson never changed jobs was because of her fantastic colleagues. They had a unique camaraderie, and she always had a smile on her face every day. She would often meet some of them outside of work too, for coffee or lunch. Going to work was not just about earning a living; it was also her social moment of the day.

As she got closer to retirement, Mrs. Everson couldn't help but wonder how her life would be after leaving her job. She was afraid of feeling lonely, spending most of the day in the house without seeing many people or interacting with friends. The thought of it was scary and filled her with anxiety. In the last few months before retirement, she found herself worrying about what the future might hold. She started questioning if she had enough interests and hobbies to keep her engaged and fulfilled during her retirement years. The fear of loneliness loomed over her, casting a shadow on what should have been a joyous transition into a new phase of life.

However, once she retired, Mrs. Everson decided to take matters into her own hands. She didn't want to let fear dictate her life. Determined to make the most of her retirement, she began to explore new opportunities to stay socially active and mentally stimulated.

She joined a local book club, which was something she had never done before. At first, she felt a bit nervous, stepping out of her comfort zone, but the ladies in the group welcomed her with open arms. To her surprise, she discovered a newfound love for reading. Discussing books with her fellow club members ignited a spark within her, and she found joy in exchanging thoughts and ideas. Moreover, she decided to try out the local gym when an old friend invited her for a free trial. Initially, she worried about being surrounded by young, fit individuals, but she soon realized that the gym was a diverse and inclusive community. People of all ages, shapes, and fitness levels came together, supporting each other on their health journeys. Mrs. Everson found that exercising was not just about physical health but also about mental well-being.

As she became more involved in the community, Mrs. Everson's life blossomed in ways she never imagined. She formed strong bonds with her book club friends and gym buddies. They shared laughter, encouragement, and life stories, becoming an essential part of her social circle.

Retirement became a time of self-discovery and personal growth for Mrs. Everson. She no longer felt the fear of loneliness that had once haunted her. Instead, she embraced the opportunities that retirement offered. Her days were filled with reading captivating books, engaging in stimulating discussions, and staying active and healthy at the gym. Looking back, Mrs. Everson realized that life didn't end with retirement; it was just the beginning of a new and exciting chapter. She had transformed her retirement years into a vibrant and fulfilling period. With an open heart and a zest for life, she showed others that age was never a barrier to finding joy and purpose. Mrs. Everson became an inspiration to many, proving that retirement could be the start of a beautiful and fulfilling journey

CHAPTER 64 Loving Adventures

Jared and Steve are celebrating their 45 years of marriage. They met when they were in their twenties. Steve fell for Jared as soon as he laid eyes on her, while it took Jared a while before being interested in Steve. She was not interested at first but then slowly started to appreciate his personality, his sense of humour, and most importantly the fact that they both loved traveling the world and always looking for new adventures and places to explore.

Before getting married and having kids they would travel and go camping or hiking in wild places once a month. They loved it. Once they got married and had kids it was harder for them to plan these activities, but they decided to have at least one, every single anniversary. They went all over the world; they rarely went to hotels. What they enjoyed was being in contact with nature and developing a connection with it, waking up in nature, the feeling of escaping the distraction and commitments of city life, and more importantly, it gave me a boost of adrenaline. Visiting wild places, sometimes even dangerous ones, made them feel alive. They always felt rejuvenated after these trips.

Over the years they slowly started to appreciate more places that offered less excitement and more quietness. they would not go for dangerous and safe places, but they would pick quiet, romantic, and peaceful locations. They would start to love sitting in the sun while reading a book or simply doing nothing.

In fact, for their 45th anniversary, they decided to leave the city, to go to the countryside, in a very isolated Airbnb. They spent a few days enjoying the nice weather, the great company and the quietness and sense of calmness that the place offered. Jared said "Honey, we are getting older" while sipping tea sitting on the porch of the Airbnb and added "We used to love wild adventures...look at us now, how much we changed."

Steve replied, "I love this quietness! but I am not going to lie, I think next year we can try to plan something wild, like the old days".

"Are you sure your knees can handle that?" Jared replied.

"Of course, I am in great shape" replied sarcastically Steve.

"Yeah, yeah" replied Jared, smiling.

CHAPTER 65 Jennifer and Cat

Jennifer and Cat are two close friends. They met years ago as they were both working for the same company. Jennifer is the kind and quiet kind of girl, while Cat is blunter and louder.

Years later they work in different jobs, and they do not see each other often. Even though they do not see each other often, their friendship is still strong and every time they see each other it feels like they never spend time apart, they just click.

One day, Cat texts Jennifer if she wants to grab some lunch together. Jennifer accepts.

As they meet in the restaurant Jennifer tells her friend that she just changed jobs and she works in the building next to Cat's job. Cat says " Wow! That is amazing news!"

"It is! I will be able to have lunch with you every day!"

From that day, they started to have lunch with each other every single day, at the usual place. One day, only Cat shows up there and she asks the waiter "Have you seen my friend today?"

The waiter replies" she told me she went to the dentist and was told to eat on the other side, and she walked away and went towards the restaurant in front of us".

CHAPTER 66 "I saw that too…"

Charlie and Alexis are a lovely couple. They live in the suburbs, and they both love the quietness and peacefulness that the place offers. Before getting married they used to live in the city, with their parents. They met through mutual friends years back and Alexis thought Charlie was not particularly intelligent at first, but then she fell in love with his personality and genuineness.

They moved recently into the new house, and they are getting used to the fact that they do not see their friends and family as often. Alexis often says, "I love it here, but I miss my friends".

Charlie is more of a laidback kind of guy, always smiling, and genuine, and seems impossible for his inner peace to be troubled.

His wife sometimes calls him "Stupid" in a jokey way because Charlie sometimes seems to be in his world and loses focus quite easily.

It is evening and after a long day at work they are having dinner, pasta, and chicken, while watching the 8 pm news together. At some point, the images show a man about to jump from the 10th floor of a building, in the city where they both grew up. They are both staring at the TV.

Then Alexis says "I think he is going to jump"

"No way honey! That would be crazy" replies Charlie.

"Do you want to bet one week of laundry, cooking, and dishes that he will?"

"Deal" replies Charlie.

After a few seconds, the man jumps off the building and they are both in shock.

Charlie says " I cannot believe that! That is horrible"

His wife saw Charlie quite shocked by what he saw and hugged him; and then said " Honey, I must be honest. I saw the same news earlier today and I knew he was going to jump. So, you do not have to do the dishes, cook, and do the laundry".

"I saw that too…" replied Charlie "… but I did not think he would jump again."

CHAPTER 67 Eggs

In the refrigerator, there are a few eggs that start talking to each other. It is 8 of them and they share their story of how they ended up there. One says, he was made on a farm in a different country and then sold to a supermarket, one said that was made and was spending time with many brothers and sisters but then they all were taken away from different men and they have not seen each other since.

One says "I wonder where we will end up…"

Another reply " I have been here for a few days and there were two eggs here that disappeared, I am pretty sure that child that opens the refrigerator ate them…"

They are all terrified hearing this story and they go quiet.

After a while, one of the eggs notices another egg and suddenly starts to be even more worried and asks: "hey, what happened to you?"

"What do you mean?"

"It's weird that you're all green and you're full of hair… Do you feel okay? I have never seen anything like this before, maybe you caught some strange disease?"

"I am a Kiwi, stupid!"

CHAPTER 68 "Where is my hearing aid?"

Once upon a time, in a cozy nursing care home, a delightful group of elderly women formed an inseparable bond over their shared love for watching TV. Among them were Margareth and Maureen, who were always seen side by side, making the most of their evenings together. One evening, as the ladies settled down to watch a movie, Margareth noticed that Maureen seemed unusually quiet and still. With a twinkle of concern in her eyes, Margareth observed her dear friend, who had a tendency to doze off during the shows. Sure enough, halfway through the movie, Maureen's head tilted to the side, and she fell fast asleep on her chair. Margareth couldn't help but chuckle at the familiar sight. She had seen this before, and she knew it was only a matter of time before Maureen's gentle snores would join the soundtrack of the TV show.

But then, something caught Margareth's attention. As she gazed at Maureen, she thought she saw something peculiar in her ear. A tiny glimmer of doubt crossed her mind, and she couldn't resist the urge to investigate further. With a touch of concern, Margareth gently woke Maureen up and leaned closer. "Maureen, my dear, I couldn't help but notice something in your ear. Are you alright?" she inquired, her voice laced with care.

Maureen blinked groggily and looked at her friend with a touch of confusion. "Something in my ear? Oh, you must be mistaken, Margareth. I'm just fine," she mumbled, still a bit drowsy from her short slumber. Margareth, however, was persistent. She leaned even closer, peering intently into Maureen's ear, and said, "No, really, Maureen. There's definitely something in there. Let me take a closer look." Maureen's eyes widened as she felt

Margareth's gaze on her ear. She reached up and touched it, trying to see if she could feel anything unusual. "Well, I don't feel anything," she said, still sounding perplexed. With the resolve of a detective on a mission, Margareth pressed on, "Just hold on, Maureen. I'm going to figure this out." She grabbed a magnifying glass from the nearby table – it was her makeshift detective tool – and peered into Maureen's ear with all the seriousness of a seasoned investigator. After a few moments of intense scrutiny, Margareth dramatically exclaimed, "Ah-ha! I've found it! There's definitely something in there!" Maureen's eyes widened, and she looked even more bewildered. "What? What is it, Margareth?" With a theatrical flourish, Margareth revealed, "It's a bug, Maureen! A tiny little bug has taken up residence in your ear! But worry not, my dear, I shall save you from this pesky intruder!"

Maureen's expression turned from confusion to a mix of surprise and amusement. "A bug in my ear? Well, that's a first! What do we do now, Detective Margareth?" she asked, playing along with the whimsical investigation. Margareth put on her best serious face and said, "First, we need to get you a hearing aid to help you listen out for any bug chatter! You know, just in case they start plotting something sneaky." Maureen burst into laughter, her sleepiness now forgotten. "Oh, Detective Margareth, you've cracked the case! But I must admit, a hearing aid might not be such a bad idea. It'll come in handy for eavesdropping on juicy gossip too!" The two friends giggled like mischievous schoolgirls, finding sheer delight in their impromptu detective adventure. From that day on, "Detective Margareth and the Curious Case of the Bug in Maureen's Ear" became a running joke among their little group.

As the days passed, Margareth and Maureen continued to share laughter and joy, their friendship growing stronger with each passing moment. Their TV-watching nights became even more entertaining as they added their own witty commentary to the shows, and they often found themselves in fits of giggles. The bug-in-the-ear incident was just one of the many cherished memories they created together, and it became a tale they shared with anyone who would listen. The nursing home staff often found themselves chuckling at the antics of their dynamic duo, and the joy spread to the entire community.

131

And so, in the heartwarming halls of the nursing care home, the bond between Margareth and Maureen became a beacon of love and laughter, reminding everyone that friendship and humor could brighten even the dullest of days. With Margareth as the ever-vigilant detective and Maureen as her witty accomplice, they journeyed through life's adventures, embracing the unexpected twists and turns with open hearts and laughter. For in the company of true friends, every day is an uplifting tale, and every moment is an opportunity for laughter and joy. And as the sun set on another delightful day at the nursing care home, the laughter of Margareth and Maureen echoed through the halls, lighting up the hearts of everyone around them. For in their friendship, they had found the sweetest gift of all – the gift of happiness that comes from sharing life's funny and uplifting moments, bug ears and all.

CHAPTER 69 The Beauty of The Sun

Sarah set the alarm for 7 am. She got up as soon as the alarm went off and opened the curtains to let the sunshine in her house. The sun was brighter than usual. Rising high in the sky, illuminated Sarah s house and garden in bright colours. The trees outside her house were particularly green, the sky was bright and blue with no clouds in the sky. It looked so nice that seemed like a portrait. She could feel the warmth of the sun on her face and that feeling gave her good humour and made her smile. Her mood depends on the weather, and every time she wakes up with nice and sunny weather, she always feels more energetic as if the day in front of her has some magic in it and looks full of possibilities and hopes for great things to happen.

The brilliant light of the sun surrounded her as she went outside. Light penetrated through the trees' leaves, creating fascinating designs on the ground. Sarah closed her eyes and took a deep breath almost as if she wanted to take a mental picture of that lovely moment.

She decided to go for a walk in a park nearby, where she was surrounded by the usual buildings that today seemed to have something special about them. The sunflowers moved slowly in the cool breeze with their faces looking up at the sky.

Sarah looked for a quiet place in the park and laid a beach towel on the grass. Her face shifted so that she could enjoy the rays of the sun. As she had her eyes closed, she heard kids playing and laughing not far from her. She opened her eyes and saw these two brothers, presumably twins, laughing, running, and kicking a ball. They were there with her mother who smiled politely at Sarah as they made eye contact. Sarah closed her eyes again and tried to feel at ease and peace while enjoying the moment. Those moments of stress-free, just feeling one with nature is her favourite part of the day. It always made her feel so good. Hearing those kids' careless attitudes reminded her of when she was a kid and the happiness she felt in her heart. It reminded her of how easy and smooth her childhood was and how lovely it was to wake up every morning and not have to deal with issues and adult life commitments.

The day went on, and she spent most of the time relaxing and enjoying the weather. She took out from her purse a small notebook where she normally takes notes of what to do during her day and writes down ideas that come up in her mind.

When the sun started to set, she got up and made her way home feeling fresh, rested, and at peace like rarely she ever felt. It was such a rejuvenating day for her. The warmth of the sun had a positive impact on her, reminding her of life's basic joys. She decided to make an effort and try to embrace the sun more, promising herself that from that day forward she will make an effort to come back to the park more often. The sun not only made her feel good but also made her think about her mindset and made her realize she should enjoy those basic things in life.

CHAPTER 70 Four Engineers

Jonathan, Tom, Matthew, and Dan are four friends. They studied together at the university. They studied engineering but specialized in different fields. Jonathan is a mechanical engineer, Tom is a chemical engineer, Matthew is an electronic engineer, and finally, Dan is a computer engineer.

It's summer, and they've arranged to go for a weekend together to the beach to have fun and get away from the daily grind.

While they are on the road they are laughing and joking when at one point, the car gives trouble and the engine dies. Then Jonathan who studied mechanical engineering says, "I knew it, it's definitely the crankshaft's fault."

Tom shakes his head and says, "No no, I'm sure it's the battery acid's fault."

Then Matthew intervenes and says, "No guys trust me…it is definitely the electronic control unit, it must have failed."

The guys try to figure out what the problem is and are extremely concentrated and concerned about figuring out how to fix it. While they are extremely focused, Dan, who studied computer engineering says, "But what if we try to get out and then get back in the car, maybe it works."

CHAPTER 71 The Magical Necklace

Nanny Lucy is putting to be her grandson, Robert. As usual, Robert asks her Nanny to tell him a story before falling asleep. Lucy is always happy to do that, and she starts;" Once upon a time, there was a small village in the mountain, the village only had a few hundred people. For many centuries there was a strange story that had been passed down through the years that mentioned something magic…"

Robert was already lost in his Nanny story waiting to hear what the story was.

"… the story was about a special necklace with the ability to give its possessor one desire. The necklace was gold and had a few bright diamonds. It was worth a lot of money. Everyone for centuries looked for it, but nobody found it.

One day Emma, a young mom, and Teema, her 13 years old daughter went for a walk by the lake. They were playing "skipping rocks" by throwing little rocks in the water trying to make them bounce off the water's surface. While Teema was looking for a small rock she saw something just under the water and asked her mom what that shiny thing was. Her mom removed her shoes, walked into the lake, looked at it, and noticed that it was a necklace. As she grabbed it and cleaned the mud out of it, she noticed that it was the necklace everyone has been looking for. She started jumping around, she was incredibly happy, she explained to the daughter the story of that necklace and they both started dancing and laughing out of joy."

"Emma spent the following day looking at the necklace thinking what wish she should make. After weeks of wondering what to decide she finally got to the conclusion that the power of the necklace should not be used for something personal, it would seem selfish to her eyes. Therefore, she decided to wish that everyone in the village would heal from their diseases, and nobody would get sick for the next 5 generations".

Robert said "Wow, so what happened? Did it work/"

Lucy continued her story " Her request was straightforward yet deep. The following morning a miracle seemed to have happened in the village. people that were in wheelchairs started to walk, blind people started to see, and everyone seemed to feel amazing. Emma was extraordinarily happy, she did not say her wish to anyone, afraid that someone might break into her house to steal the necklace."

Then, Lucy continued " The necklace represents hope and the love for our species. Emma could have wished for something that would have improved her life drastically. She always dreamed of having a massive house by the lake, but she could not afford it. This story shows that kindness can be extremely powerful and that acts of kindness for other people can have huge consequences in the community. It is not necessary to wish for everyone to feel better or heal their diseases to make an impact."

Lucy finished her story and then wished goodnight to Robert. She aimed to teach him kindness and the importance of thinking about others. She always used stories to educate her kids and she is doing it now with her grandkids.

CHAPTER 72 An Embarrassing Story

In a nursing home, a few ladies are telling each other some embarrassing stories of their life.

As they are laughing and thinking of old stories one of them said "I think I have the most embarrassing story…" and so she started to tell her story

"I remember that I was in second grade, and I had to give a presentation in front of the entire class. I was very shy, and it was a big deal for me. I spent the night before rehearsing and hoping for the best. I could not sleep. The following morning surprisingly, I felt calmer, but as the clock was ticking, I started to feel more agitated and nervous. So, a few minutes before my presentation I went to the toilet. I was trying to tell myself that everything was fine, fortunately, there was nobody in the toilet and I started to feel more relaxed until I looked down at the buttons on my skirt. At that age and feeling extra tense and nervous my mind went blank, and I didn't remember how to button my skirt properly."

Her friends start laughing as she tells them the story. She laughed with them and continued "I left the bathroom convinced that nothing would happen if I didn't button it. Convinced that my skirt would hold up. I started the presentation and felt extra confident, I started well. I was surprised, I loved that I was able to explain everything as I studied it. Everything was going great, and I started to feel extremely confident. A few minutes later I saw a couple of girls laughing, but I did not pay attention. Then I see other guys laughing and then the whole class. I looked around and then I looked down…it happened. My skirt slipped to the floor."

Her friends at the nursing house burst into a big laugh. and she continued:

138

"I was so embarrassed that I wanted to disappear, I wanted to cry, I felt so nervous and shocked that my vision was blurred, I could not hear anything, my mind went blank. Everyone was laughing…"

"OGM, I am so sorry to hear that, that must have been traumatic," one of her friends said."

"It was, my best friend tried to cheer me up, but I just wanted to disappear. The idea that everyone laughed at me made me feel sick. However, I think that after that I started to feel more confident going into other presentations because I thought "Definitely there is nothing worse than this…" fortunately, at school, people made fun of me only for a short while, then there was the summer break, and everyone seemed to have forgotten about it".

CHAPTER 73 "I am your uncle..."

"It was my mom's birthday and I was there with my boyfriend. Plenty of people were there, most of them were family members' ' Sophie said as she was having brunch with her friends.

Lucy says, "How was it?"

"It was so great up until…" and then Sophie started laughing.

Her friends giggled and said, "What happened?"

Then Sophie said "I was quietly sitting on the sofa and my boyfriend was next to me. Then, I was just so focused on watching the kids play at the back and a few moments later I grabbed my boyfriend's hand who in "theorywas next to me and whispered: "tonight you are going to get lucky". I heard a voice saying "excuse me…"

"Who was it?" asked her friends.

"My uncle…I wanted to disappear."

They all started laughing then Sophie said "I was so embarrassed, and he was too, he became all red, and then I apologized, but I could see he was probably more embarrassed than I was. He is my uncle; he saw me growing up".

"This is too funny," her friends said.

CHAPTER 74 "Mom, where did you put the frying pan?"

Henry is a 24-year-old guy from a small village near Chicago. He moved out a few months ago from his house and went to New York, where he is sharing the apartment with another girl that was already living in the apartment.

His parents go to New York once every three or four months to visit their son.

The first time they went there, his mom, Grace, was excited to see the city and to see her son. She is a very protective mom that treats her son like a baby even though he is now a grown man. When Grace and Micah, Henry's parents, saw their son they were super excited, they liked the place, and they were very happy to see him happy.

After a couple of hours, his roommate, Caroline, showed up. They all had dinner together and spent a lovely time together.

On their way back home, Grace told Micah "I think they are together" and Micah replied "Oh, do not start with your imagination, they are just roommates."

"I know my son...I am sure they are dating; I picked up a vibe."

After a few months, they went to visit their son again and when they left, Grace was sure, his son is definitely dating the girl.

A few months after that, they go back to New York for a couple of days. After they see their son and spend time together, Grace pulls Henry into the kitchen and asks, "Are you two dating?"

"No, absolutely not," replied Henry.

Two days later Caroline asks Henry "Did you see the meat frying pan?"

"No, I did not, my mom used it to cook. I am going to ask her where she put it".

So, Henry calls his mom and asks her where she put the frying pan, Grace replies: "If Caroline slept in her bed, she would know it is under her pillow…I knew you two are together".

CHAPTER 75 Fortune Teller

A woman goes to a fortune teller and asks for information about the future.

Fortune teller: "Good evening, madam, how can I help you?"

"I found out from a friend of mine that you can see the future...is that true?"

"Yes, what is the name of your friend?"

"Aurora, she is an Italian girl."

"Oh, sure Aurora. She's a great friend of mine" and then he adds "How can I help you? What exactly do you want to know?"

The lady is a little wary and does not know whether to tell the truth or be a little vague, so she decides to stay general at least for the beginning, until she gets a little more confidence in the guy.

So, she says, "I'd like to know a little bit about what my future will be like at the work level, will it be better or worse?"

The fortune teller after asking for some information and pulling out a few items says, "You have a bright working future ahead of you, you're going to get some great news soon."

"Oh, that's great news" replies the lady who then asks a few specific questions about it.

Next, the fortune teller asks, "Is there anything else you want to find out?" and then adds, "I perceive a great event in your life."

"Positive or negative?" replies the lady.

The fortune teller says, "I see a great misfortune: your husband will die."

"I know that, but do I care if the police will do an investigation?"

CHAPTER 76 "Can I please have two tickets?"

Luc is an American guy that is on vacation in Italy. He found out from a friend that he can buy the ticket on the bus and does not need to do that before. So, he is waiting for his bus and after a few minutes, the bus comes. He gets on the bus and asks the driver: "Morning, can I please have two tickets?"

The driver, confused, says" "What do you need two tickets for, since you are alone?"

"If I lose the first, I have the second one. Just in case".

The driver smiles and says in a joking way:

"What if you lose the other one too?"

"No problem, I also have the monthly ticket."

CHAPTER 77 Ticket Inspector

A group of guys wants to go out for a party. They are all in their twenties and love going out and having fun. Thomas is supposed to drive them to the party, but just before leaving the house, he noticed that his car has some issues, and the engine will not start. So, they decide to go to the club party they are heading to on the bus.

While they are on the bus, one man gets on the bus and shouts "Nobody move! Give me all your money!"

One of the guys said " Oh I got scared! I thought it was the ticket inspector".

CHAPTER 78 "Do you remember what happened?"

Larry and Daphne have been married for almost 5 years. They do not have children yet, and they live in Ohio.

After dinner, they are watching Netflix on TV. It's the usual evening for them, they enjoy watching TV shows and movies together.

The following morning Larry finds himself in the hospital, in very bad shape, with his head bandaged and one hand in a cast. As soon as he is back in a conscious state, the doctor asks him, "How are you?"

"I feel a little dazed...what am I doing here?"

"He lost consciousness, now he is better. He is in the hospital. Do you remember what happened?"

"My wife and I were sitting on the couch and watching her favourite TV series. At one point I asked her to bring me the chocolate bar, but she refused. Her cell phone rang in the kitchen. She immediately got up to see who it was and found my message, "Since you are already in the kitchen, you can bring me the chocolate." After that, I don't remember anything. "

CHAPTER 79 Nice Weekend

Dave, turned to his wife, Susan, with a mischievous grin. "Do you want us to have a nice weekend?" he asked, wiggling his eyebrows suggestively.

Susan chuckled, not sure where Dave was going with this. "Of course!" she replied, playing along with his antics.

Dave dramatically paused for a moment, as if contemplating an elaborate plan. "Then I'll see you on Monday," he declared dramatically, pretending to walk away. Susan burst out laughing, rolling her eyes playfully. "Oh, come on, Dave! You can't be serious!" she said, trying to hold back her giggles.

Dave turned back to face her, his eyes sparkling with mischief. "Oh, but I am serious!" he exclaimed dramatically, striking a superhero pose. "I have planned the ultimate surprise weekend extravaganza!"

Susan raised an eyebrow, intrigued. "Oh, really? Do tell!"

Dave leaned in closer, lowering his voice conspiratorially. "First, we'll start with a secret mission to find the world's best pizza. I've been researching pizza joints all over town, and I've got a map with hidden treasure marks."

Susan laughed, shaking her head in amusement. "You and your love for pizza! Alright, I'm in."

"But wait, there's more!" Dave continued, pretending to be a game show host. "After our pizza adventure, we'll head to the beach for a sandcastle-building contest! I've been practicing my castle-building skills in the backyard."

Susan couldn't contain her laughter. "You've got to be kidding me! This is going to be the most epic weekend ever!"

"You bet it will be!" Dave proclaimed proudly. "But there's one more surprise, and this one's the best of all. Are you ready?"

Susan nodded eagerly, unable to wipe the smile off her face.

"We're going on a top-secret, covert operation to raid the ice cream parlor!" Dave said, now whispering like a spy. "I've got insider intel on the best ice cream flavors, and we're going to taste-test them all!"

Susan burst into fits of laughter. "Oh, Dave, you're incredible! I can't believe you've planned all this."

Dave wrapped his arms around Susan, pulling her into a warm hug. "Well, you deserve the best weekend ever, my love," he said tenderly. "And I promise you, it's going to be a weekend full of fun, laughter, and unforgettable memories.

And so, Dave and Susan embarked on their whimsical and hilarious weekend adventure. They searched for the best pizza, built sandcastles like kids at heart, and indulged in an ice cream feast that left them both with the happiest of brain freezes.

As they laughed and enjoyed each other's company, they realized that the key to a truly delightful weekend was not extravagant plans or expensive outings. It was about embracing the joy of spontaneity, letting go of everyday worries, and relishing in the simple pleasures of life together. From that day on, Dave and Susan made a pact to have "surprise weekends" regularly, where they would take turns planning whimsical and funny adventures for each other. Each surprise weekend became a cherished tradition, strengthening their bond and filling their hearts with love and laughter. And so, Dave and Susan lived happily ever after, making memories that would keep them smiling for a lifetime. Their love was a beautiful symphony of joy, humor, and heartfelt affection, proving that the most extraordinary weekends are the ones crafted with love, laughter, and a dash of silliness.

CHAPTER 80 Storm in The Village

Chloe was a cheerful girl who lived in a village in the mountains. The village that during some months of the year is nothing short of heavenly. One day in the summer while the kids are playing outside, the women are gossiping and preparing food, while the men are watching sports on TV, a big storm hits.

Everyone had to come back home. The storm was so violent that there was no longer electricity. Everyone was very worried that the storm would devastate the village and the gardens that had vegetables.

Once the storm passed Chloe decided to go for a walk with her best friend Jared, they walked around the mountain. As they were walking, they noticed something not far from them. They could not tell what that thing was, but it looked like a big box, in the middle of the forest, just sitting against a tree.

They walked around that area very often and had never seen that before. It must have been brought there by the storm.

They got close and the closer they got they realized that it was not a normal box, but it looked like a safe.

The two girls tried to open it but failed to do so, so they came back and told their parents about it. Their dads followed them through the forest to see what their daughters were talking about, hoping they did not make anything up and feeling hopeful it could be something special.

The village was devastated, and people were desperate, so they needed that to be good news.

As soon as they opened the safe, they were blown away. There was gold inside, a lot of gold. They could not believe their eyes. The box was extremely heavy, and they needed to call a couple of other people to bring it to the village.

They sold the gold, made so much money to pay for all the damage the storm causes, and much more. Every single family in the village became financially stable, and nobody worried about money anymore. They all enjoyed life without needing to work.

CHAPTER 81 "I Love You"

In a nursing house, a few ladies are telling each other stories. One of them is telling her friends about her first boyfriend. She goes:

"I used to live by the sea, I was 17 at the time. I invited him to the beach in the evening to go for a walk and spend some time with him. The weather was beautiful. It was extremely sunny, very warm and the sound of the sea hitting the beach was the perfect background".

Teo came on his stunning motorcycle wearing an orange helmet, which I loved, a white shirt that was partially open, and his jeans shorts still-ripped pants... anyone would have envied his physique. He was buffed."

"Oh, I love this story already," says one of her friends.

"I was there at the beach, dressed in a long black dress and standing in a pair of slave sandals. I felt excited and nervous at the same time. We were dating for only a couple of weeks at the time, and we were in the "honeymoon" phase. He looked perfect in my eyes, he was so beautiful, smart, kind...he seemed perfect to me."

Then she added "We spent some time just walking on the beach. I normally love walking on the beach only if my feet are not wet. Once they get wet, I hate the feeling of the sand on my feet. While I was with him though, I did not care at all. It felt like time stopped, there was a magical feeling in the air."

"That is a wonderful date, I have never been on a date like this. That seems to be coming from a movie" another of the ladies said.

"I would miss him when I got home, and when we got home in the evening, we would text each other until late. He was very sweet to me. The following evening, we did the same thing, but he took me to a restaurant first and then we sat on a bench by the beach."

She smiled, stopped for a moment, and then carried on.

"He had just smiled at me and kissed me on the head while sitting next to me and said: "Hello Laura, why did you invite me?" while smiling". I felt very excited and a bit nervous around him. I was very shy as a teenager."

"That is so adorable and cute," said a couple of ladies while listening to the story.

"I went silent for a bit trying to find the right words and then I said, "I do not know… that is the place where we first met, I wanted to spend some time with you." and he said, "I miss you, too." I could feel my cheeks becoming red… he took my hand and looked into my eyes, and he said, "I love you". I was ecstatic, smiling, and in the process of emotion, I had begun to cry. I replied, "I love you too."

CHAPTER 82 Life

I ended up in the emergency room for a big bump on my head, had blood everywhere, and a towel pressed to the cut that wouldn't stop throwing. I'm the queen of bumps because I'm careless, which is why I didn't even want to go to the emergency room. I didn't see the bump on my head, but the wide-eyed people who took one look at it persuaded me that maybe a trip to the hospital was in order.

At the counter, the nurse's apathy reinforced in me the swaggering notion that it must not be such a big deal after all, even though by now the towel was soaked and I was dripping everywhere under the astonished eyes of the other waiting patients. By the time I was convinced she was going to discharge me with a reproachful glare for wasting her time and a diagnosis of a bump led me to mend.

On a gurney was a body so old and worn out by life that, on impact, I couldn't tell if it was a living thing with all those shrunken wrinkles on that exposed chest with no more modesty, perhaps skins that once contained breasts but I'm not sure. From the tiny stature, I then thought it was a woman, a little woman. An old woman of the tiny kind. That gaunt thinness, those forlorn skins on the bones made me feel so sorry that I almost apologized and went home. Please, this way. As if the old woman wasn't there.

What could I do as if she wasn't there? What hypocrisy had taken hold of me? I did everything not to look that way, not even caring that they would patch me up. Finally, the nurse pulled a sheet to separate me from that view, so I could at least relax my gaze. But I didn't stop thinking about the thing resting beside me, with a few strings to monitor how much life remained in it at the bottom.

I let it stitch me up, tame. All I thought about was how far I was from the bottom, from having such a helpless body, and how much I had left to live before my life had to be measured in remnants.

One last look before going out to that chest, this time I wanted to make sure the chest, yes, was moving, breathing. Why? Why did I bother? The little old lady was being cared for, although I didn't see a bustling around her. Why did I make sure she was breathing, why did I want to violate that moment with that last look?

I began a countdown, took possession of the decay of that body, used it, robbed it to count, to count how much time I have left, how much life I can still pull up from the bottom of my well before I am pitied as a thing laid there to give up life.

CHAPTER 83 Old Memories

One day Elizabeth was cleaning her old room and found an old box. She opens it and sees many papers. She slowly begins to read them one by one: papers from when she went to school as a child and various drawings. At one point she notices a poem. A poem was written by her when she started writing poetry as a young girl:

Naked,
  lying on the bed,
  Stripped even of every thought,
  mute and devoid of all desire.
  Between my sighs
  And the sound of rain
  I see you lying there.
  Your smile.
  Tell me again!
  I looked at you,
  you stared at me.
  Your stories
  Can make me take flight.
  Tell me everything,
  don't go away
  And when you're done,
  start again.

CHAPTER 84 Music

Michael is a teenager who loves music. His passion does not come from his parents, neither of them is a musician. He loves music, but unlike his friends, he sees music with a deeper meaning, it is not just sound to him It is life. One day he decides to write a poem about it:

A gentle melody delights the hearing,
    Your sweet face colours the dress.
    A brushed harp seems like a magnet,
    your enamoured hair adores your fingers.
    Music is blissful and heavenly.
    contact with the supernatural,
    formidable relief at all hours,
    escape valve against all pain.
    And you are a content of rapped notes,
    rhythm gushing forth and traversing expanses,
    enchanted harmony of subtle voice
    roared the emblem of vinyl magic.

CHAPTER 85 Almost Love

I am at the bus stop; I'm outside waiting for the bus. Here it finally comes the bus.

The stream of people coming down collides with the one going up, as I climb the step, I feel myself being pulled from the opposite side. I see the thread of a shirt caught inside the zipper of my bag. I look up and see her, our eyes meet halfway, staring at each other for an indefinite time.... she is beautiful, anything a regular guy like me can dream of.

Now, in the most classic of romantic stories, we would have fallen hopelessly in love. My gaze screams, "Eh no shit! At the risk of leaving a hole in your shirt, I'm not getting off the bus!"

While she seems to be thinking, "Eh no, at the cost of taking 'this sucker' with me, I have to get on the subway!"

With two fake smiles, we try to get the thread out of the zipper. Meanwhile, the last people get on the bus, anxiety rises. I feel like a thief who is looking for the combination to open the safe, as footsteps down the corridor approach the door only to turn into a spinning knob.

Fortunately, an old lady, who was laughing and giving us directions in the meantime, intervenes, and with a simple movement, she practically pulls the wire in the only direction we had not tried.

Sighing in relief, and smiling, she and I look at each other again... My look serenely says to her, "See you never again!"

And hers, "Finally this nightmare is over!"

CHAPTER 86 Future is Bright

9.10 at the bus stop, the cold morning air nipping at my nose. I had layered myself up like an Arctic explorer, wearing so many clothes that if anyone dared to stab me, they would barely get through the eighth substrate shirt. Three teenagers stood nearby, chatting and laughing, seemingly unfazed by the chilly weather.

As I waited for the bus, the tallest among them, a well-built guy, turned his attention towards me and erupted into giggles. "What the hell are you wearing? You look like Santa!" he exclaimed, his friends joining in on the laughter. I felt a pang of embarrassment, unsure of how to respond to their teasing remarks. Trying to brush off their comments, I chose to ignore them and focused on staying warm. After all, my ultimate goal was to reach my destination without catching a cold. I couldn't let a group of teenagers with a penchant for teasing ruin my day. However, my momentary discomfort was soon overshadowed by the arrival of a petite and particularly thin girl, her presence commanding attention. With her flowing blond hair and bright red lipstick, she exuded confidence and charm. She was dressed in a daring outfit, a mini skirt that was more mini than a skirt, paired with a light white shirt and a short, thin jacket that offered little protection against the cold.

The boys greeted her warmly, their playful teasing shifting towards her choice of attire. Unfazed, she folded her arms to protect herself from the biting cold and justified her outfit choice with a bold declaration, "These stockings cost a whopping forty pounds, and I thought they would be enough to keep me warm!"

Her response earned chuckles from her friends, who admired her fashion bravado. But the unexpected happened when the big guy, the same one who had mocked me earlier, chivalrously opened his large jacket, inviting the petite girl to find warmth under it. She accepted the offer with a coy smile, and he enveloped her in his embrace, holding her close. Her head rested gently on his chest as they shared a tender moment amidst the chilly morning. The envy in their friends' eyes was undeniable. It was evident that they all admired and appreciated their blonde friend's presence and charisma.

To everyone's surprise, the big guy locked eyes with the young girl, and without any hesitation, they leaned in for a sweet, unexpected kiss. The sight left their friends in jaw-dropping astonishment, their playful banter temporarily silenced.

As they exchanged affectionate glances and tender gestures, the guy suddenly shifted his attention back to me, wearing a sly grin on his face. "I bet you're a virgin, don't look at me!" he taunted, trying to get under my skin. In that moment, I couldn't help but feel a mix of emotions. I wanted to stand up for myself and respond with a sharp retort, but I decided against it. Instead, I chose to rise above his hurtful words and maintain my composure.

Years flew by, and life took its course. Many experiences shaped me, molding me into the person I am today. As fate would have it, I found myself driving a sleek Lamborghini, with my gorgeous fiancé seated beside me. We passed the same old bus stop, and there he was, the same guy who had once mocked me, now looking disheveled and melancholy. The sight tugged at my heartstrings, and I couldn't help but feel compassion for him. Life had its way of teaching us lessons, and sometimes, it humbled us in ways we never anticipated. As I glanced at my fiancé, a sense of gratitude washed over me. I had found love and happiness, and that was worth more than any petty mockery.

The moral of the story remained unchanged: life as a teenager could be tough, filled with insecurities and uncertainties. But it was also a time of growth and learning. As we journeyed through life, we faced ups and downs, but the future held boundless opportunities for happiness and success. And so, I chose to cherish the beautiful moments, like the unexpected bond between the young couple at the bus stop, and let go of any bitterness from the past.

As we drove into the horizon, my heart brimming with hope and positivity, I knew that the future indeed held endless possibilities. Life had taught me to be resilient and to embrace the bright and promising days that lay ahead.

CHAPTER 87 A portrait of two people

Sitting next to me on the train seats is a young girl. Her face is hidden behind her hair and her hands are half covered by the sleeves of her shirt. She pulls a pad of small sheets of paper and a fine-pointed pencil out of her bag. In front of us, a boy and a girl are sitting fixed on opposite sides, their faces looking sullen. They look very serious. I do not think they know each other. If they do, they are not on good terms as they are completely ignoring each other.

The young woman at my side begins the hatching by lightly drawing a series of curves. She points her pencil inside them and makes it go up, takes a slight curve to the right and then to the left, goes up some more to swerve right again, and ends up in a kind of horizontal oval.

Curious, I follow the delicate movements of the pencil on that rough paper. She is making a portrait and she seems to be very talented in my opinion. On the right, she draws a window, and she then also puts thick curly hair to her face. I look at the girl in front and realize she is drawing her.

The girl with the big hair is looking out the window and the talented girl next to me draws her perfectly. A few minutes later I notice she is drawing the same scene, but this time with her gaze turned not outward but toward the boy. And she draws him too, both with a cigarette in her hand, his head resting on her shoulder. His jacket, her shirt, her hair, and her facial features as in front of a mirror she interprets are all very similar. The girl keeps drawing, and she also creates a small table, where the two rest their hands with cigarettes, the side window becomes a classic house window, and the boy is shown as if he grew a beard. To the girl instead, she gives short lines at the sides of the eyes and above the lips. They have aged. She points the eraser at one of these lines and begins to erase and then stops; she then reconsiders and puts the line back on.

The voice from the loudspeaker announces the stop, she tears the paper from the pad and gives it to the girl. "Hi, I'm Kirstie, and this is for you."

Kirstie smiles, puts her magic tools in her bag, and leaves.

The curly-haired girl stands there with the paper in her hand, the boy turns curious to look at the drawing. The two old men on the paper draw, this time, two smiles on the lips of the couple who now look at each other and laugh.

"What are we? Look how many wrinkles she gave me, and we don't even smoke… that's nice, though."

He takes the paper out of her hands and puts his head on her shoulder; they both try to make the same expressions and have the same posture in the illustration. They started laughing. Then, they stop and remain silent, staring at the drawing without saying anything more. This time the pencil is wielded by their thoughts, and they are reproducing those same features in each other's heads, making them imagine that future together.

A portrait of a stranger improved the atmosphere between the couple that started laughing. Sometimes small actions can have powerful consequences.

CHAPTER 88 "Hey honey"

There is a girl I often meet on the bus back from work. I remember the first time I saw her (or at least noticed her), the bus was packed, I was seated but stood up and I invited her to sit down. She smiled, thanked me, and sat down. She was beautiful and she had a sweet smile.

One day we even exchanged a few words about the missed bus ride. She also got off at the same bus stop, heading for the subway station. Me in front and her a few meters behind me. She was on the phone. I intentionally slowed down to mind her business and find out if she had a boyfriend. Yes, I admit it!

This was the conversation:

She said, "Hey honey".

My mind stopped. I am a hopeless romantic and already picture me and her together. When I heard "honey," I thought she was talking to her boyfriend. I could not hear what the other person said.

Then she said "Of course, I am free tonight, I cannot wait to see you."

After that, they started talking about their day at work and I could not tell who she was talking with. Then she repeated "I cannot wait to see you tonight" and she added "Usual romantic place?".

My heart stopped.

I was already walking in the other direction when I heard "Okay see you later! Ask Mom and dad if they want to join us too. Love you, sis".

I was incredibly happy, I walked towards her and said "Excuse me, I am sorry to bother you. You probably do not remember me, but I saw you on the bus and I wanted to let you know that you look absolutely beautiful".

She smiled and said "Of course, I remember".

We started talking and exchanging numbers. We went out the following night and kept dating for a while.

CHAPTER 89 Job Interview

Job interview.

"So, we would start with 1,000 euros per month and after 6 months we would go to 2,500 euros per month."

"OK, I start in 6 months."

CHAPTER 90 The Wise Man

It is said that in an ancient kingdom, lived a man known everywhere for his wisdom. He was a very old man, in his 90s. Nobody knew exactly how he acquired that level of wisdom, but everyone seemed to be blown away every time he spoke. At first, he gave advice only to his family and close friends. His fame, however, grew to such an extent that the king himself began to call him often to ask his advice about personal problems and to ask him questions about the kingdom and politics.

Every day many people came to receive his valuable advice. However, the sage noticed that various people came to him every week and told him about the same problems over and over again, so they always received the same advice but did not put it into practice. It was a vicious circle.

One day the wise man gathered all those people who often asked for advice. Then he told them a very funny joke, almost everyone burst out laughing. After waiting a while, he told the same joke again. He continued telling it for three hours.

In the end, they were all exhausted. So, the wise man said to them, "Why can't you laugh many times at the same joke, but you can cry thousands of times over the same problem?"

CHAPTER 91 Friends in the Desert

Once two great friends decided to cross the desert. They trusted each other and felt they could not ask for better company. At some point during the journey, the two had a difference of opinion about a specific and not-so-important conversation. It was probably the tiredness and fatigue that made them more prone to arguing.

From disagreement, they moved to an argument and from that to a heated debate. The situation degenerated to the point that one of the friends punched the other. The latter immediately realized his mistake and asked for his forgiveness. Then, the one who had been hit wrote in the sand, "My best friend hit me."

They continued their way until they found themselves at a strange oasis. They had not yet entered when the ground began to move. The friend who had been hit began to sink. It was a kind of swamp. His friend reached out as far as he could, risking his life, and saved him.

Just then the boy who had been hit and then saved wrote on a stone, "My best friend saved my life." The other looked at him curiously, so he explained, "Among friends, offenses are put in writing only for the wind to carry them away. Favors, on the other hand, should be engraved deeply so that they are never forgotten."

CHAPTER 92 Superb Lion

A superb lion was very hungry. He had not eaten for a while now and his stomach was growling, but he knew that where he lived there were not enough animals he could eat, especially at that period of the year. He had not eaten for hours, and considering his size as well, he desperately needed food.

He understood that he had to be patient and cautious while hunting since if a prey came along and he lost it, he would not easily find another.

The lion remained quiet behind a bush. A few hours passed and no prey presented itself. When he had given up hope, a hare appeared nearby. There was a pasture, and the hare came out to eat some grass, not paying attention. Aware of the hares' speed, the lion knew he would have to make a sudden and decisive attack. Otherwise, the hare would run away.

He waited a while and stood at attention. When he was about to pounce on his prey, he suddenly saw a beautiful deer walking a few meters away. His mouth watered. In a couple of seconds, he changed his mind and attacked the deer, which, however, had time to see him and start running. The lion then turned and ran toward the hare, which, hearing the lion run initially toward the deer, had run away.

This story teaches that it is better not to let go of what represents a certainty for us in exchange for something that suddenly seduces us.

CHAPTER 93 Christmas

The Christmas period is surely one of the most beautiful, not only for what it can represent in its historical event but for the magic that always surrounds it.

For children, it is certainly experienced on the level of magic among songs about Christmas, lights, tall trees lit up, streets with a thousand glittering storefronts, and wishes visible to all behind glittering windows. For adults, enthusiasm in giving things to their children, children present at home, but also a lot of nostalgia. In short, around the Christmas table, there will be empty chairs, although present in the heart.

I was very fortunate. I had a happy childhood or at least I keep this memory.

My mom always made a big Christmas tree quite brightly lit that ended with a very tall finial. My brother and I were always very careful not to break it by passing the glass balls and we would check that the star was always firmly planted on the last branch at the top.

A lot of work in short to make all this and to put it back afterwards. I still keep all the boxes with those old characters, today made of other materials, but for me, unsurpassed.

I remember always spending the 24th evening at my grandma's and leaving a few biscuits and milk in the kitchen for Santa. The same night, once we came back home, the biscuits were not there anymore, and the milk was partially drunk by Santa who left my gifts and a note for me. I was always so happy to open gifts, it was such a beautiful moment that I miss.

While Santa used to give me clothes like dresses, shoes, and coats. The Befana was for toys and dreams. The Befana is on the 6th of January. We never celebrated in the UK, but my dad being Italian brought this tradition into the family.

The evening of the 5th when we were already in our beds my mom would prepare sweets, dried fruits, toys, and invariably my very tall, beautiful chocolate-coloured doll with black curly hair which she took out of the big box in her closet, where she usually stayed, every year to make her live in those days. I remember being very happy to have her in my arms, taking her to the movies and in the stroller.

All this is no longer used of course, but, to me, it taught me a lot, such as taking care of one's belongings and also tidiness not only that, because the fact that after sixty years or so my historical memory is still alive and present I think is not only due to the head but also to the heart and soul that have clutched to them a stainless essence.

CHAPTER 94 Never Give Up

Matthew is a 15-year-old kid. He loves football, people say he is talented. His dad always supported him and despite him not being a football fan he always followed his son and watched his games.

Matthew plays for the local team, but one day he has the chance for a trial in the biggest team in the city. His dream is becoming a reality, he is about to sign a professional contract. However, the day of the trial he realizes that the level of the team is very high and that it is very hard for him. At the end of the training, the coach lets him know that he did not pass the trial.

Matthew was disappointed and very sad. He did not talk the whole day. His dad tried to cheer him up, but it seemed impossible. So, the following day, the dad wrote a letter for his son and left it on his desk. The letter said:

Never tire of working for a better world.
May tomorrow always be better than today.

Don't listen to those who try to extinguish your dreams.
Forget that person, his dreams have already been extinguished.

But keep dreaming and create your ever-better tomorrow.
Don't look at what you don't have but look at what you do have.

Don't look at the defeats but look at the victories small or big.
One step at a time we can climb the mountain.

The future is ahead of us.
  The past is past, gone.

Do not hold back the shadows of the past.
  Those also darken the future.

The future is in front of us,
  Good or bad this depends on your decisions and what you do now,
  And it depends on each of us.

After reading this poem Matthew decided to pursue his dream even more. Years later he finally signed his professional contract and started playing football all over the world. The power of encouragement from one's parents is the biggest form of support to believe in one's dreams.

CHAPTER 95 The Star Stella

Once upon a time, there was a star named Stella, which lit up every night in the sky along with all the other stars: they had a very specific task, they were to look down on the earth to check through the windows that all the children were sleeping peacefully in their cribs, in the company of teddy bears, puppets, and dolls.

One evening Stella had almost finally finished observing each little house beneath her when she noticed that a window filled with light. What was going on in that room? There was someone not sleeping, and it was very late!

Intrigued, she approached with a stronger beam and saw a little girl crying sitting on her crib. Stella then shone even more, to get the little one's attention, but the baby continued to cry.

The good little star did not give up and called for help from the other stars next door; she asked them to shine even brighter and in different colours.

They all agreed, if they could make the little girl stop crying and, suddenly, the night sky turned into a great dark carpet embroidered with millions of sparkling lights. Also, the little girl's room lit up with a thousand colours: the little finally noticed it and raised her eyes in amazement at the final window.

Stella approached her to ask why she was crying.

"I cry every night because I am afraid of the dark!" the hopeful little girl answered her.

Selene then explained to her that she should not be afraid because every night all the stars would light up in the sky just to make sure the children fall asleep peacefully. The little star promised her, moreover, that she would stay longer above her limit. So it was, and the little girl from then on had only sweet dreams.

CHAPTER 96 What a Special Couple!

Elizabeth is now a grandma, and she is in her 80s. She is up to this day full of energy and loves telling stories of her life to her grandkids. One day, her oldest, Maria, comes by her house for lunch. Maria tells her grandma that she feels a bit nervous as in a few days she will meet her boyfriend's family. She only met her boyfriend's sister, but she has not met her parents. She says "I feel very nervous. I hope they will like me".

Elizabeth replies "Do not be silly, of course, they will".

"I do not know it is not just his parents but his grandparents, uncles, and aunties..."

"Where are you meeting them?"

"We will meet at his grandparents' house. They always plan a big lunch in the summer every year and this year I am invited."

"Honey, that will be a magical moment that you will always keep in your heart and mind. Enjoy it! Trust me. I have been there. I wish I could go back and relive it".

"How was it for you to meet Grandad's family?"

Elizabeth started telling her story. Grandad overheard it, interrupted her and full of enthusiasm asked to tell the story himself. Elizabeth smiled and agreed.

"Your grandma was the most beautiful girl I have ever seen; her eyes were shining like the sun. Her ..." and Elizabeth interrupted him and said, "You do not have to tell her the story of our life..." and everyone smiled.

So, Grandpa and Grandma started telling the story together and kept laughing, and giggling and went on for a long time reminding each other of episodes of the time they met each other's family.

Maria loved it and looked up at her grandparents hoping one day she could have the same and hoping she would get married and have a long and happy marriage.

CHAPTER 97 Kindness

Elena and Sara were two inseparable friends in their small Canadian town. As they strolled through the park one day, they noticed an elderly man struggling with heavy shopping bags. Elena compassionately remarked, "Look at that poor person, he looks like he needs help."

Sara nodded in agreement, her caring heart urging her to act. "You're right, we should offer him a hand. Let's at least carry the bags to his house," she suggested.

Approaching the old man, they kindly asked, "Good morning, sir. Can we give you a hand with your envelopes?"

The old man, whose name they soon learned was Tom, smiled gratefully and accepted their assistance. During their walk, they discovered that Tom was alone and had no close relatives to lean on for help. Upon reaching his home, Tom expressed his heartfelt gratitude. "Thank you so much for your help, girls. I am very grateful for your kindness."

Elena and Sara replied in unison, "It was a pleasure to help you, Carlo. Remember, we are here if you need anything else."

From that day on, the friends made it a point to visit Carlo regularly. They not only brought him food but also kept him company, listening to his stories and making his life less lonely. As the weeks passed, their bond grew stronger, and the trio formed a beautiful friendship. Elena and Sara's acts of kindness had made a significant impact on Carlo's life, bringing light and joy to his days. Their selfless acts of kindness not only brightened Carlo's life but also inspired others in the community. As news of their compassion spread, more people joined in, offering their assistance and friendship to the elderly in their town.

Their simple act of helping an old man with shopping bags rippled into a wave of compassion and support, creating a tight-knit community where everyone looked out for one another. Elena and Sara's friendship became a beacon of hope, showing that through small gestures of kindness, they had ignited a chain reaction of love and care that brought warmth and joy to the hearts of many. The two friends were thrilled to see how their actions had sparked a positive change in their community. They realized that kindness was indeed contagious, and it had the power to bring people together and make a difference in people's lives.

Inspired by their experience with Carlo, the two girls became even more passionate about helping others. They joined local charity organizations, volunteering their time and effort to support those in need. Whether it was distributing food to the homeless or organizing community events, they always made sure to spread kindness wherever they went. Their acts of kindness were infectious, and soon more of their friends and acquaintances joined them in their mission to make the world a better place. The small town started to flourish with acts of compassion and camaraderie, creating an environment where everyone felt cared for and loved.

As the years went by, their friendship remained as strong as ever. They continued to make a positive impact on their community, leaving a legacy of love and kindness for generations to come. Through their journey, they learned that being a true friend meant more than just having fun together. It meant being there for each other in times of need and reaching out to those who needed a helping hand.

Their story was an inspiration to many, a reminder that a simple act of kindness could change someone's life and ignite a ripple effect of goodness in the world. And so, Elena and Sara continued to walk hand in hand, spreading love, joy, and kindness wherever they went. Their friendship became a shining example of the power of compassion and how it could transform not only individual lives but also entire communities. As they looked back on their journey, they realized that their friendship had grown stronger through their shared experiences of giving and caring. They knew that they had found a lifelong companion in each other, someone with whom they could share not only laughter and joy but also the beautiful gift of making a difference in the lives of others.

In a world where negativity often seemed prevalent, Elena and Sara's story was a beacon of hope, a testament to the profound impact that kindness and friendship could have. They had shown that no matter how small an act of kindness may seem, it had the power to change lives and create a brighter, more compassionate world for all.

And so, their journey of spreading kindness and making a difference continued, as they walked hand in hand, leaving trails of love and warmth wherever they went. Their hearts were full, knowing that their friendship had not only enriched their own lives but had also touched the lives of countless others, making the world a better place, one act of kindness at a time.

CHAPTER 98 Honesty

Bernardo and John were two friends from childhood. They met at school as children. John was initially stupid by the fact that Bernardo had a different accent and was from another country. One day, while they were playing in the schoolyard, they saw a wallet fall out of the pocket of another child, Festus. John took the wallet and looked inside. There was money and an ID card.

Bernardo said, "John, what are you planning to do with that wallet? We should give it back to Francis. That's the honest thing to do."

John looked at the wallet and pondered for a moment. Finally, he decided to follow Bernardo's advice. Together, they went to find Festus to return the wallet to him.

When they found Festus, they told him, "Hi Festus, did you lose your wallet? We found it in the schoolyard."

Festus became agitated and said, "Yes, I lost it! Thank you so much for finding it. I was desperate!"

Bernardo and John returned the wallet to him, and Festus was so happy that he wanted to reward them with some of the money inside. But they politely declined.

John said, "We only did what was right. Returning your wallet is the most honest way for us to behave."

Festus was relieved and said, "You are two really honest and good guys. I am happy to have you as friends."

From that day on, Festus, John, and Bernardo became inseparable. They learned that honesty is a core value that creates solid bonds between people.

The moral of this story is that even though it can be tempting to keep something that does not belong to us, it is important, to be honest and to give back what we do not deserve. Bernardo and John demonstrated that honesty is an action that leads to trust and true friendship.

CHAPTER 99 Ladybug

Once upon a time, there was a little girl named Louisa who gave her.

grandfather Leo a tiny fake ladybug, just like a real one. It looked very real, it was all red, covered with dark dots, with a little black head and tiny antennae.

Grandpa put it in his coin purse, which he always carried with him, and every time he opened it, he saw the little ladybug thought of his granddaughter, whom he loved very much. Unfortunately, he could not see her often, because the little girl lived far away with her parents, so they had invented a game: every time they would phone each other, they would tell each other that the ladybug had travelled between the two houses and they would say to each other, "She is here with me now, tomorrow she will come to you!" Thus, it seemed that the ladybug travelled a lot, when in fact it did not move from Grandpa's purse.

Meanwhile, as the years went by, Louisa was growing up and began to go out more with friends and to call her less often to her grandfather. But he knew that as she got older her granddaughter would become a little detached from him, and he did not mind. However, every time he opened the coin purse, seeing the ladybug he kept thinking of her.

One day, as he was watching her, it seemed to him that she was moving: "How is this possible? "Grandpa thought. Then he looked closer, the ladybug was moving up toward his hand: it was alive! The ladybug with a subtle little voice said, "Now I'm going to Louisa!" and flew off.

Grandfather knew nothing more about her for two days, still amazed at that magic. Then, needing money, he opened his purse, and at that same instant, the ladybug landed again on his hand.

"I've been to Louisa's, and I bring you her greetings," she told him, then went back into the coin purse to rest. The ladybug had acted as a messenger between grandfather and granddaughter, making both happy.

CHAPTER 100 Lesson from Dad

"A blind man, with his white staff, in the middle of the desert cries without being able to find his way because there are no obstacles," the father said to his son.

The son was complaining that ever since he finished college, he has had one problem after another: with his girlfriend, with work, with the football team…. the father responded with that sentence explaining to his son that the blind man must dodge obstacles to move forward. They are a barrier for him, but they are at the same time a point of reference. He discovers this only when they are gone.

At the same time, the same is true for everyone. Obstacles often direct us to a better future or help us improve.

CONCLUSION

In conclusion, this book was created with the intent to stimulate the mind, have an enjoyable time, and make elderly readers feel good. The stories in this book were carefully chosen to offer a variety of experiences ranging from laughter to smiling and reflection.

Through these stories, I hoped to bring back the experiences of the elderly's past, allowing them to reconnect with precious memories and share joyful moments. I am convinced that the smiles elicited by these stories are lasting memories that will accompany them on their life journey.

In addition, the book aims to convey a positive message about the lives of the elderly. The elderly has accumulated an abundance of wisdom and experiences that can inspire and teach all generations. I hope that through these stories, readers were able to reflect on how precious time is and were encouraged to embrace each moment with gratitude and joy.

I thank all the readers who chose to share their time with this book. I sincerely hope that this book brought laughter, reflection, and moments of serenity into the lives of those who read it. Reading these stories has been an opportunity to relive past emotions, find consolation in laughter, and feel connected to a community of people who appreciate and value life.

In conclusion, I hope that the stories made people think and laugh, bringing joy and serenity into the lives of the elderly. May it be a valuable gift for all who seek a moment of inspiration and enjoyment. I wish all readers a life full of happiness, health, and precious memories.

Made in the USA
Las Vegas, NV
05 January 2024

83913252R00108